Real Estate Investing Gone Bad

21 true stories of what NOT to do when investing in real estate and flipping houses

By Phil Pustejovsky

ISBN: 1523269030
ISBN-13: 978-1523269037

Table of Contents

Introduction

"A smart person learns from his own mistakes. A wise person learns from the mistakes of others."

Most real estate investing books describe all the wonderful financial benefits that occur when everything goes right. There is certainly much to learn from success, but what about all those situations when things don't turn out as planned? What about all those real estate deals that went bad?

What you're about to read are 21 true stories of real estate deals that went terribly wrong and the lessons you can learn from them. The cost of these lessons to the effected parties totals millions of dollars in losses, years of unproductive activity and incalculable emotional stress. However, you'll obtain the enormous benefits of the lessons they learned without the costs. Therefore, what you will gain from this book is infinitely more valuable than the price you paid for reading it. You're about to gather lifelong, extremely valuable real estate investing lessons that have taken others a lifetime and a fortune to learn. This is what NOT to do if you plan to be or are already a real estate investor.

However, the intent is not to scare you away from investing in real estate either. Although some of the losses you will discover are absolutely devastating, hopefully you will not become so frightened by them that you run from real estate altogether. But instead, the goal is for you to gain new insight on how to make wise investing decisions in the future.

The collection of stories in this book is the most extensive research project on real estate investing failures ever. First, all of my own real estate "war" stories were collected from the thousands of deals I have personally been a part of, as well as all the people I have interacted with over the years who have shared with me details of deals that have not turned out the way they planned. Second, I reached out to the most seasoned investors across North America that I personally knew and gathered stories from them. Third, with my #1 YouTube channel on real estate investing and one of the most visited websites for investors, I asked my audience of hundreds of thousands to share the details of their worst deals.

After two years of assembling a gigantic archive of stories, I then poured through them all and chose the ones that had the greatest losses and the biggest lessons. Furthermore, there were plenty of stories that had the same lesson, but different circumstances with different people in different places. In such situations, a definitive story that best encapsulated the lesson was chosen. In the end, this collection represents the best of the best stories from the most ambitious quest for real estate investing horror stories ever accomplished.

Disclaimer: Although the following are based on true stories, to protect the anonymity of the parties involved, names and even some minor details have been changed as to prevent readers from reverse engineering the exact deals and participants.

1. Non-Refundable Earnest Money Deposit

Brand new to real estate investing, Jerry was anxious to do his first deal and didn't want to wait long to do it. Jerry had been networking with anyone and everyone and somehow got on the email list of an out-of-state wholesaler. One day, he got an email from that wholesaler about a property that looked to be the deal of the century. It was a house that could be worth $130,000 once fully renovated that was for sale for only $60,000. After viewing the property, Jerry could see that it needed to be renovated extensively, but there was still a huge potential profit in the deal from his calculations. Jerry was thrilled and thought to himself, "Finding a deal isn't as hard as everyone says it is. Heck, these great deals find me!"

In order to finalize a contract with the wholesaler, Jerry was required to provide a $3,000 non-refundable earnest money deposit. The wholesaler assured him that it was customary and normal for transactions with this much potential profit to require 5% upfront to execute a contract. Jerry mailed the check to the wholesaler and then after the contract was executed by both parties, it was sent to a local closing firm to prepare for the closing.

Jerry, meanwhile, wanted to get a head start on the project and sent a contractor over to the property. He also contacted a real estate agent to help him better determine what the property would sell for once it was all fixed up, as well as what rehab work was most critical to getting the highest price.

His excitement changed when his agent said that it probably wouldn't sell for more than $100,000, even if was in perfect condition. The $130,000 potential value Jerry had in his head had come from the wholesaler. It was a value that his agent explained was far too optimistic for the area the house was located in. Furthermore, the contractor discovered several issues that Jerry had overlooked and the cost to renovate, even if they used the cheapest grade materials was going to run more than $30,000. All of a sudden, the deal didn't look so good and he considered backing out.

He stood to lose $3,000 if he walked away. Rather than walk away from that money, he chose to buy the property. He financed the purchase using a home equity line of credit from his primary residence. He hired a different contractor who told him the work could be done for far less than $30,000.

When the work was supposedly done, he hired a different agent who suggested that listing it at $124,900 would get the house sold in a matter of days. But after several months, the house had not sold. Not even one offer came in. The few showings it did have provided feedback that the house needed too much work. "Too much work?" thought Jerry, "How, on Earth, could the house need more work? It was just fully renovated!"

Jerry fired his agent, blaming her for being lazy, not holding any open houses or trying to get an offer from the people who did see it. He began to blame the economy for his woes, complaining that the market was slow in that area.

Meanwhile, the interest payments on his home equity line of credit were starting to really eat into his finances. So, he arranged to refinance his investment property and pull the cash out that he had used to renovate the house to pay back the home equity line of credit.

Frustrated with the lack of buyers, he put the property up for rent and immediately had tremendous interest. He was relieved to finally have some positive news on this property.

Soon after the tenants moved in, they began to report problems. There were all kinds of issues, from peeling paint, to leaks in the plumbing, to electrical problems. It soon became apparent that the contractor who had renovated the house had cut corners everywhere he went.

Jerry was losing money every month due to the maintenance issues. Eventually, the tenants were so fed up with the problems, they stopped paying the rent. Jerry had to evict them, which cost him thousands more in lost rent, empty mortgage payments, and legal fees.

When the home was finally vacated, he had to hire another contractor to redo the paint with primer this time, as well as replace the carpets that the tenants had destroyed, and fix any other issues the original contractor had created.

Now nearly two years since the original purchase, Jerry again had the property up for sale. This time though, he just wanted to get rid of it and recoup his loses. Unfortunately for Jerry, the market had actually dropped and houses were selling for less than when he had bought it. He watched as the list price had to drop further and further until he finally got an offer at $90,000.

Jerry calculated that in the end, he had lost more than $23,000 and the property had taken up years of his life. In reflecting, he thought back to what he could have done differently....

He could have taken the $3,000 loss and backed out of the deal altogether. It would have saved him over $20,000, years of his life and enormous amounts of stress.

He could have hired the original contractor even though that person was not telling Jerry what he wanted to hear. And, he also could have listened to the real estate agent who predicted it wouldn't sell for more than $100,000. (It dawned on Jerry that working with real estate professionals that don't always paint a rosy picture may be the ones that are the most accurate in their advice.)

Instead of blaming the agent, the economy or the market, he could have simply dropped the list price from the original $124,900, down to an amount that would have generated an offer.

Rather than refinancing, which tallied up thousands in extra fees and expenses, he could have just sold the property by dropping the list price to free up his home equity line of credit.

Rather than resorting to renting a property that wouldn't sell, he could have figured out why it wasn't selling and fixed that problem rather than creating a new and larger problem.

Better yet, he could have NOT agreed to non-refundable earnest money. Perhaps he could have negotiated 7 days for due diligence in which to back out so that he wouldn't have had to potentially lose $3,000 to begin with?

This story plays itself out quite frequently. It all began by agreeing to non-refundable earnest money with no due diligence period. But that was just the beginning because that mistake alone wasn't the most serious decision that set the rest of the problems into motion. Ultimately, the biggest mistake Jerry made was paying too much for the property.

When someone pays too much for a property, like a pebble dropped into a still pond, it ripples outward over a huge area. There isn't enough room in the deal to pay a quality contractor so the work is done sub-par to meet the inadequate budget. The property must then be listed higher than it should to compensate for paying too much for the property. Then, when it doesn't sell, the listing agent is blamed.

Sadly, if a buyer does purchase a property that has been renovated poorly (to compensate for the investor paying too much), the buyer is buying a home that has underlying issues which may not rear their ugly head until months or years after moving in. Thankfully, in this example, Jerry had to sleep in the bed he had made by being the landlord responsible for any maintenance issues.

In the end, the real blame should be on the foolish investor who paid too much for the property and put that domino effect into motion.

Powerful and Profitable Learning Lessons

(1) Have an inspection period before your earnest money deposit becomes non-refundable so that you can back out if you discover major problems that drastically reduce the potential profit in the deal.

(2) Don't ever base your investing decisions on the estimated after repaired value or fix up cost the seller of the property provides you.

(3) Never assume a piece of real estate will be worth more a year from now than it is today. Although real estate usually appreciates in value, there are certainly exceptions based on local changes as well as larger economic adjustments.

(4) Don't buy properties with very thin profit margins because it can (a) prevent you from being able to afford renovating the house at the required standard of quality; (b) push you to list the property for sale at a price far above market value; (c) force you to turn it into a long-term rental; and/or (d) tempt you to refinance into a long-term loan with significant loan origination costs.

(5) When buying real estate that you intend to renovate and resell, also known as "flipping", always purchase at a price that is low enough to have a margin for error built in. Your estimates of how much it will cost to fix up as well as what it will sell for once the property is renovated, may be wrong. Having a built in margin of safety will reduce the problems that may come when an estimation mistake is made. Warren Buffett's first rule

of investing was to not lose money. His second rule was not to forget the first rule.

Do you have additional questions about this story? Go to www.realestateinvestinggonebad.com to ask a question about this story or any other story you read about in this book.

Phil Pustejovsky

2. The Two Lost Deals Caper

Ben was eager to do his first deal. He had read as many books as he could get his hands on, attended every seminar that came to town, read online articles and watched videos for hours each day, and had spent his life savings on courses and trainings. Along his travels, he ran into an investor named Victor who was also a hard money lender. Victor seemed like such a nice guy because he offered to fund deals for people like Ben who found great deals but didn't have the financial wherewithal to purchase them.

For months and months, Ben tried to apply what he had learned about finding good deals and he kept running into bad deal after bad deal. "Finding deals is *MUCH* harder than they say it is," thought Ben. But Ben was not a quitter and so he kept at it. After nearly 9 months, he finally felt like he had found a homerun deal. The seller was extremely desperate to get rid of the property because he was going to prison and didn't want to make empty house payments while he was incarcerated. Before Ben made an offer though, he wanted to make sure he had the money to buy it so he called on Victor for help with funding the deal. After Ben provided as much information as he knew about the deal, including contact information of the seller to go inspect the house, Victor gave him the green light that he would fund the deal up to $150,000.

The seller was hard to reach, making last minute preparations before going away for a while, but once Ben caught up with him, he made the offer of $150,000 and the seller asked if he could sleep on it. The next day, to Ben's surprise, the seller informed him that he had chosen to sell to another investor who offered him more. Ben was devastated. All that time and all that effort had come down to this one deal and now it was lost, swooped up by some other investor.

Ben thought long and hard about whether or not he should even continue with real estate investing. Maybe it wasn't for him? He knew the road less traveled wasn't going to be easy and there was going to be bumps and bruises along the way so he committed to keep going. He also gained a little encouragement in knowing that at least the first deal that he lost was a good one because someone else took it. He knew what a winner looked like now and if he did it once, he could do it again.

It was another long 3 months of hard work before he found another potentially great deal. This time though, his plan was to make an offer right away, and not waste any time. He made the offer to the seller, but the seller wanted some time to think it over. While he was waiting for a response, Ben contacted Victor and asked him about funding this deal. Ben was thrilled to get the approval of Victor to fund it. Unfortunately for Ben, the seller stopped returning calls or emails. The seller had basically disappeared.

Ben was completely deflated. Here was his second legitimate deal in 9 months of hard work and it too had slipped through his fingers. Although this one seemed to be a different problem, the seller had just vanished.

As persistent as Ben was, he was also having difficulty explaining to friends and family why it was smart to continue to do something that after nearly a year of consuming all of his thoughts, energy and money, had produced no results whatsoever. In fact, his father pointed out that if Ben had spent all that time working at McDonald's rather than fiddling with real estate, he would have earned thousands of dollars (as opposed to shelling out thousands for courses and trainings). It was a hard pill for Ben to swallow. As much as he hated the idea of giving up on his dream of being a real estate investor, he felt he had given it his best shot and it just didn't pan out for him.

A few months later, thinking back over his brief career in real estate investing, he wondered whatever happened to those two great deals he had found. Doing a little online research, he found out that the same LLC had bought them both and subsequently sold them for tens of thousands more. It was incredibly painful to see with his own eyes that he was so close to making a ton of money but yet someone else had made that money. Who was behind this LLC? He further researched who that lucky investor was who owned that LLC and he about fell out of his chair when he saw the name...Victor! He couldn't believe it. The hard money lender had stolen both of those deals from him!

Victor handed Ben an old-fashioned lesson in how it works in the real world of real estate investing. Great deals are very hard to come by and if the deal is not completely locked up correctly, it can easily get taken. Local investors who position themselves as hard money lenders are notorious for stealing deals from wholesalers who aren't smart enough to have their deals locked up. Sellers show no favoritism or loyalty either, and will sell to whomever can give them the most money the fastest. In Ben's two deals, Victor knew what the offer was and the address and simply went to the property and offered the seller slightly more than Ben did.

Ben felt betrayed by Victor and disgusted by real estate in general. If that's what the real estate business was like, he thought, then he wanted nothing to do with it anymore. Ben never again ventured back into the realm of real estate investing.

Most unfortunate for Ben was that had he gotten those two deals locked up with the right paperwork before reaching out for funding, he would have made a tremendous amount of money. And, from those two initial deals, may have become a lifelong, very successful real estate investor. But instead, he didn't recognize the lessons and it forever changed the course of his real estate future.

Powerful and Profitable Learning Lessons

(1) Great deals are hard to come by. Make the most of them when you find them.

(2) When you have a great deal on your hands, lock it up with a contract and also, preferably a recorded instrument, to ensure no one can take the deal from you. Then, you can look for money to purchase it.

(3) Don't give up on real estate, even if you meet with temporary setbacks. Those initial lessons you learn from the mistakes you make can be the foundation for a prosperous career in the business.

Do you have a deal gone bad story of your own? We want to hear about it! Swap real estate investing war stories at www.realestateinvestinggonebad.com

Phil Pustejovsky

3. The Grass is Not Always Greener

In certain areas, the prices for real estate are much higher than in others. And, for those real estate investors that want to own income producing properties but live in very high priced areas, it can be very tempting to look for greener pastures far from home. Gina was just that type of investor. She wanted the benefits that owning real estate long term could provide for her; from consistent monthly cash flow, to appreciation, to tax write offs in the form of depreciation, the increase in equity from tenants paying down the mortgage balance with each monthly rent payment, and maybe even some appreciation that real estate often exhibits.

She thought she had stumbled upon a wonderful solution to her problem; buying properties in other markets that were already rented and already had a property manager in place. Oftentimes referred to as turn key properties, these deals only required a new buyer and supposedly everything else was already handled. Since they were already leased, it helped with obtaining mortgages and within a few months, she was the proud owner of a property over 500 miles away. She had put down 20% and her calculations estimated a return of 8%, which was much better than she was getting from her other investments. The best part was, she had enough money left over to buy 3 more properties just like it. If she tried to purchase something locally, she could have barely purchased one property.

The grass is not always greener though. The tenant stopped paying rent and Gina began making empty house payments while learning how the eviction process worked. It turned out that the lease had been missing several key clauses and it took an extra few months to legally extract the non-paying tenant from the property. Plus, they left the property a wreck. The property manager lined up a contractor who charged thousands to re-carpet and re-paint the property along with a few other renovations.

Gina got her calculator out again and realized that it would take 3 years of cash flow just to payback all that she had lost from this one tenant moving out. She experienced firsthand just how costly a vacant single family rental can be to the owner and also how overly optimistic her 8% return assumption was for this deal.

She decided to just sell it to immediately recoup her losses. She was shocked to discover that what she had paid for the property was far more than what it would sell for on the open market. She had been so focused on how cheap the total price was in comparison to the prices of real estate in her hometown that she didn't bother to consider the purchase price relative to the actual market value of the property. Since the properties in Gina's hometown were priced 4 times higher, it gave her the illusion that what she was buying was a good deal simply because it was ¼ the cost of a property in her local area. Instead, she was learning the hard lesson that the difference in price between what you can buy a property for in your hometown versus in another area doesn't determine safety of investment. It is the actual market value of that specific property as defined by comparable sales of similar properties nearby relative to the purchase price.

It also began to dawn on her why the seller of the property was selling to someone 500 miles away rather than to someone in the local area. They well understood the maxim PT Barnum coined, "A sucker is born every day." Due to the relatively high rental rates in comparison to property prices (and by adding a 4th bedroom), the previous owner was able to sell the property for more to a long distance (unfamiliar with the local area) investor as a turn key rental than to a local retail buyer looking to move in to make it their family home.

Gina was also puzzled by how the appraiser the lender hired when she bought the property could have appraised it for the full purchase price when just 9 months later, she couldn't sell it for anywhere near what she had paid for it. She learned another good lesson. Appraisers will often use the contract sales price as a major determining factor in what the property appraises for. Therefore, she learned that it is the responsibility of the buyer to study the comparable sales and understand for themselves what a property would sell for if it was ever to be put up on the market for sale. An appraisal doesn't always accurately determine what a property will sell for when listed on the open market.

Not wanting to lose any of her original 20% down, she opted to once again rent it. A few weeks later, the property manager provided her with two choices of tenants, and Gina felt good knowing that she had some control over the decision as to who was going to rent the property this time. And 10 months went by with no drama. And then once again, the tenant stopped paying and the nightmare started all over again. Thankfully, she had learned a few things from the first eviction so this next one wasn't as severe. But once again, there were more maintenance bills and the costs for this supposed investment were eating up her personal finances.

After a month with no tenant, she decided to fly out to the property and figure out what was going on. She discovered that the property manager was hardly even marketing it for a tenant. Gina also was shocked by how poorly the work had been done by the handyman. She saw with her own eyes the dangers of hiring people without having any way of holding them accountable.

Then, she dug deeper into the financial relationships of the parties and found that the property manager was getting a kick back from the contractor on all the work he was doing. Perhaps even worse, she looked at her agreement with the property manager and calculated that since the manager received 100% of the first month's rent, or $1,000, but only $100, or 10% for each monthly payment thereafter, the manager made more money the more the tenants changed. Even if the property sat vacant for a few months, if the property manager made 10 times more each time a new tenant moved in, they still made much more money than by having a long term paying tenant.

Gina had made several mistakes, but she discovered that she needed help. She narrowed it down to two options. She would either let it go and eventually watch it fall into foreclosure or she was going to invest what little she had left on some education to turn her ship around. She applied for and was accepted into the Freedom Mentor Apprentice Program *(shameless plug of the author's real estate investor mentoring service)* and rather than throw her hands in the air and give up, she decided to get educated on what to do with this deal and turn her previous failure into a foundation for her future success.

Her mentor guided her to take action. First, rather than re-rent to a normal tenant, she was taught to instead, locate a Tenant Buyer on a Rent-to-Own arrangement who would not only be striving to one day be the owner, but would also put up a sizable nonrefundable option payment. She discovered that although the rental market was saturated, the demand for Rent-to-Own houses was enormous and was able to quickly secure a Tenant Buyer with a $5,000 option payment who also had a good job and good rental history. That extra $5,000 was instrumental in paying her back for all the empty house payments and repairs she had to do after the last tenants had been evicted. In addition, she set an option price that would avoid her losing money.

Next, she hired a new property manager to keep an eye on the property but was able to negotiate a far reduced percentage on the monthly income and removed the ability to receive kickbacks from contractors. Then, she connected the Tenant Buyers with a mortgage broker as soon as they moved in to immediately begin work on improving their financial situation so that they could get a loan prior to the end of the option period.

A year later, she was able to sell the house to those Tenant Buyers and walk away without having lost her original 20% down payment investment as well as getting paid back all her losses. No, she didn't make any money, but in the end, she broke even financially and gained something far greater from the experience. Gina now knew how to make wise investing decisions moving forward and went on to excel as a real estate investor.

Powerful and Profitable Learning Lessons

(1) The grass is usually not greener elsewhere. Owning rental real estate long distance, even with a property manager in place, can be very difficult and is oftentimes unprofitable in the long run.

(2) The price of the property in relation to the price of real estate in your area is not an indication of margin of safety. Just because the price is low in your mind, doesn't mean it's a good investment. All purchase prices, large or small, must be compared to the market value to determine if you have purchased a property wisely.

(3) The best investments are NOT the ones that are laid out to you on a silver platter. If it's all been "done-for-you", chances are, the deal is not as good as you think. As Andrew Carnegie said, "The first one gets the pearl, the second gets the empty shell." Most turn key property deals are examples of sellers having snatched the pearls and selling the empty shells to you.

(4) Working with a mentor is the single best way to shortcut your way to success in real estate and avoid the many pitfalls that far too many people fall into.

You can learn more about the Freedom Mentor Apprentice Program at www.freedommentor.com/apprentice

4. Beware the Naked Man Who Offers You the Shirt off His Back

Jill and Linda had been best friends since college and their dream of owning their own business had come true. Nestled in an eclectic part of town, was the Eyeliner Diner, and it was booming. In just a few short years, they had also seen the area surrounding their business take off too. What used to be a dangerous part of town was now the cool place where young professionals were getting into bidding wars in order to buy houses. Jill and Linda wanted to get in on the local real estate boom.

Their plan was to buy fixer uppers, renovate them with this young professional buyer in mind, perhaps even find the buyers by posting flyers at their diner (as opposed to having to pay a real estate agent) and make a fortune by selling for significantly more than they had purchased it for and paid to fix it up.

Jill couldn't help but overhear a conversation by a regular who sat at table # 16 mentioning the phrase, "flipping houses." It was music to her ears. They got to talking with this gentleman, Rick, and Jill and Linda thought they had found a match made in heaven.

Rick would find the deals for them and renovate them too. All they had to do was bring the money and provide some direction on what colors to use to appeal to the young professional crowd who were gobbling up anything that hit the market in that area. The Eyeliner Diner consumed most of their time anyways so Rick being the deal scout and contractor was perfect for Jill and Linda.

Low and behold, a few weeks later, Rick presented the budding investors with a deal that appeared to have tremendous opportunity. Rick suggested they get an appraisal, both an as-is value as well as an after repaired value, so that they had a better understanding of what they could expect to profit. Who should they hire to appraise the property? Rick knew a guy who could take care of that for them. And that was the way it was with Rick. He had a solution for everything, including where to find the money to buy the property. Rick connected them with a hard money lender willing to finance 65% of the purchase and the renovations.

Excited about watching their plan come together, much like the Eyeliner Diner, Jill and Linda plunked down a sizable down payment and now Rick was off to work on fixing up their first house together. But even before he could finish, he had found another great deal! The second one closed even faster since they had done it once before already. Plus, trust was building with Rick and he was taking care of all the little details while Jill and Linda focused on their thriving diner.

There were some delays on the completion of the renovation of the 1st deal and would you believe it, Rick found a 3rd deal that Jill and Linda needed to jump on quickly or they would lose out. Their cash reserves were tapped out and they really needed to sell one of the other two deals to get the cash to buy the third one. Rick came up with another plan. Refinance the 1st deal into a conventional mortgage and pay off the high interest hard money loan. Rick had just the guy to help with that too. This was back in the days when the appraiser could be chosen by the lender, so the appraiser who had appraised the properties already did the refinance appraisal as well.

Jill and Linda were thrilled by how high the appraisal came in at because not only did they pay off the hard money loan and all the fix up costs, they also got their entire down payment back plus some extra money. Flush with so much cash from the refinance, they purchased the third deal. Since the formula was working so well, they eventually refinanced the 2nd and 3rd deals too.

It was just about the time that they were into the fourth deal that something began to be amiss. Why wasn't the first deal selling? They had thought that houses around there were flying off the shelves but yet their property had sat on the market for over 120 days? Also, Rick had become increasingly harder to get a hold of when they called. He always had a different excuse. And, he wasn't showing up around the Diner as much either.

With 3 conventional mortgages on the first 3 deals and one hard money loan on the 4th deal, the monthly payments were starting to significantly reduce their cash reserves. They were just about to start panicking when an offer came in on deal #1. But their enthusiasm evaporated quickly when they saw that the offer amount was far less than list price. In fact, it was less than what they owed! Bewildered, they asked the agent that had listed the property, a contact of Rick's, how that was possible? He chalked it up to just a low ball offer and to not pay attention to it. But then, the agent representing the buyer proceeded to provide comparable sales to support their offer. It turned out, the agent Rick had recommended was brand new in the business and was just as surprised as Jill and Linda when those comparable sales revealed a value far less than the refinance appraisal had shown.

Rick was once again difficult to reach during this time and now on their own to decide, they chose to accept the offer and prepare to bring money to the closing. They were further shocked to discover a gigantic list of problems on the inspection. The inspector revealed a different reality than Jill and Linda had known. It seems the work that was done was extremely shoddy, corners were cut at every conceivable turn and in some cases, the repairs weren't done up to codes. Before Jill and Linda could speak with Rick about the inspection, the buyer backed out.

At this point, Rick was not picking up his phone at all. The pair started calling the contacts they had met through Rick to try to reach him a different way, but everyone expressed the same challenge in being able to get a hold of him lately. Rick had basically disappeared. And meanwhile, they were now beginning to fall behind on mortgage payments.

Jill and Linda had seen their house flipping dream turn into a complete nightmare. They contacted several different organizations to try to piece together if what had happened to them involved fraud or anything that could deemed illegal for they felt they were victims of a terrible scheme. Frustratingly though, despite the awful position they were in, it was hard to pin down any legal wrongdoing. The appraisals, although very high, were still within the rules of an appraisal. Certainly the highest comps were used for the reports, but nothing that could be deemed fraudulent. The hard money lender had relied on the as-is appraisals but in 3 of the 4 deals, he had been paid back and on the 4th one, his 65% loan to value position was still safe for him in the event it went to foreclosure. The refinance mortgage broker had charged high origination fees but nothing completely out of the ordinary. Although Rick's quality of work was determined by an inspector to be very poor and he charged very high rates for his contracting services, technically, he hadn't done anything illegal either.

After much research, they connected the dots and realized that Rick had made a killing off of them. Each deal he found, he had wholesaled to them, collecting huge profits upfront. Then, he made a ton more money as the contractor because he grossly overcharged them. In all, they calculated that in the span of about 6 months, he had made about $150,000 off of them. As soon as all their money and resources had basically dried up, he was gone, onto the next victim.

Jill and Linda eventually filed bankruptcy and along with losing all the houses they had purchased and all the money they had put into them, they also were forced to sell their thriving Eyeliner Diner business. They learned an extremely hard set of lessons in real estate. Although it costs them all they had, they discovered some enormous lessons on real estate investing.

Powerful and Profitable Learning Lessons

(1) Do one's own valuation determination even if an appraisal has been completed because appraisals don't always equal what a property will sell for in the end.

(2) Watch the work of a contractor every step of the way because when you take your eye off of them, they can cut corners. If you don't know if something will meet codes, then find someone who does to check the work.

(3) The main lesson they learned though was bigger than those two distinctions. They learned to beware the naked man who offers the shirt off his back. They should have been highly suspicious of someone who would be so apt to not only find but also fix up supposed great deals and then let them collect all the profit. If those deals were so good to begin with, why wouldn't someone as knowledgeable and experienced as Rick have done those deals himself? The answer in this case was that the deals were only good because Rick found a pair of suckers who had money and the ability to obtain mortgages, they weren't intrinsically good deals. A fool and his money will soon be parted. Had they been actually really good deals, Jill and Linda would have never caught wind of them because an experienced person like Rick would have done those deals himself.

(4) Sadly, this situation is quite prevalent. A simple rule of thumb to remember that can help you be on guard for bad deals cloaked in "good deal" clothing is that if someone else is offering a real estate deal to you on silver platter and all you have to do is provide money or credit, be very cautious. For if the deal was really

that good, you can be assured that you would have never heard about it. Great deals rarely fall in your lap wrapped in a bow. The best deals in real estate are typically the ones you painstakingly dig up and discover yourself through hard work or superior intelligence.

Phil Pustejovsky

5. All That Glitters is Not Gold

After decades of slow accumulation, Jeremy had finally transitioned from owning single family home rentals scattered all over to concentrating his investment portfolio into two apartment buildings. It had taken 20 years to reach that level and the cash flow from the two properties were terrific. But, he wasn't completely satisfied.

As a commercial appraiser, he had been exposed to an enormous amount of real estate experiences over the course of his career and he felt there were even better investments beyond the horizon. He had heard tales from very wealthy people in the area about the "holy grail" of properties that produced extraordinary cash flow with very little management headaches. Just like he had upgraded from single family homes to apartments, he now wanted to graduate up from there.

Despite the money flowing in from the apartments, Jeremy complained to his wife about the headaches that came along with managing all those units. He had gone through several onsite managers for each property over the years and finding good, reliable help was a challenge for him. Rather than enjoying the safety from vacancy by having hundreds of individual tenants, he wanted to reduce the number of tenants he had to deal with. Jeremy felt that less would be more for him. Less tenants would be less hassles because there would be less people altogether and no need to hire unreliable people. If he wanted the job done right, he felt he had to do it himself anyways.

The other issue nagging Jeremy with his apartments were the types of tenants he was dealing with. They were residential tenants and some just didn't pay their rent on time. Due to his occupation as an appraiser, he saw the difference business people displayed in regards to paying their bills. Businesses paid bills on time because they ran businesses with bookkeepers and consistent income (unlike his average apartment dweller who couldn't balance a checkbook or keep a job if their life depended on it). Jeremy solidified in his mind that he was going to upgrade into the world of owning commercial property that leased to businesses.

An old widow contacted him about doing an appraisal on her office building. The property was beautiful; class A office space downtown along the most valuable stretch of road in the city. Jeremy had completed appraisals for her husband throughout his life and she took over the property after her husband had passed away.

This particular property, named the Icon, had just a few tenants; including a very prominent attorney and an investment bank. The marble, the chandeliers and the huge oak finishes made you feel like you were on Wall Street when you entered the building. And Jeremy was in love with the property.

He asked the widow why she wanted to do an appraisal and she said that she was looking to sell. Jeremy smiled from ear to ear. This was the opportunity he had been looking for because he knew she owned the property with no loan against it and he may be able to structure owner financing and avoid getting a bank loan. He asked her if it would be a conflict of interest to consider making an offer and she agreed that if another appraiser did an independent valuation, she'd be happy to negotiate a deal with him and avoid the commissions of listing with a broker. Plus, her late husband had known him for so many years and had only good things to say about him.

This was a classic example of an "off market" deal in commercial real estate. Jeremy recommended a fellow appraiser that he knew would appraise the property without a bias toward either party and when it was completed, the widow and Jeremy worked out the price to be the same amount as the appraisal. And at first, Jeremy planned on getting a loan.

Approaching a few lenders that he knew liked class A office buildings, Jeremy thought the loan would be easy to obtain. But he was surprised that he was turned down by every one of them. Sure, the Icon was bringing in the money the lenders wanted to see, but there were several issues that had spooked these banks. One reason was that one of the most important tenants had a lease that would be coming up for renewal shortly. The main issue was Jeremy himself. He had never owned any office buildings before. His net worth and other financial data was not as large as they wanted to see.

Undeterred, Jeremy went back to the widow and presented the idea of her becoming the bank, owner financing him, so long as he provided a very large down payment and agreed to refinance within 3 years. What sealed it for Jeremy was his impeccable reputation for having always followed through with his commitments. She agreed.

To get the down payment, Jeremy was going to have to sell the better of his two apartment buildings. His plan would be to sell and 1031 exchange the gains tax deferred into this new property. This was a high level technique learned from all his years in real estate. Far from being a novice, Jeremy was about as experienced in real estate as one could be.

Selling the apartment property would be very easy because of the very strong positive cash flow and how well he maintained it. He didn't even have to put it on the market. He simply called a few colleagues and had a full price offer almost immediately.

On paper, the math didn't look as good though. The new property he was purchasing didn't produce as much cash as the existing apartment building he was selling. Jeremy reasoned that the reduction in hassles of only dealing with a few high level tenants would more than make up for reduction in monthly cash flow. Plus, the property itself was in the very best part of the region. To use an analogy from the classic board game Monopoly, he was selling Kentucky Avenue to purchase Park Place.

When the whole deal finalized, he became the owner of the Icon by using $600,000 from the sale of his apartment building and the widow owner financed the remaining $1M. Jeremy felt he had arrived as a businessman. He walked a little taller and talked a little more confident. He had to pinch himself every time he drove by because he couldn't believe he was really the owner of the Icon.

At first, the lack of headaches from not dealing with his previous apartment building had reduced the number of details he had to manage. But then, he discovered that class A office buildings had management issues too. For example, the elevator stopped working during business hours one day. He hadn't dealt with such an issue before so he wasn't prepared for an immediate fix. Several days passed before it was finally fixed and by that time, the investment banking tenant was furious and threatening to sue for losses because a few high net worth clients were unable to use the stairs.

Having a high powered attorney for a tenant turned out to be scary because this individual could sue on a moment's notice for even the smallest of issues. It got so petty that this attorney even complained about people taking his parking spot even though there were no officially assigned parking spots for anyone. To appease him, Jeremy had a sign printed officially designating the spot for the attorney. However, then the investment bankers complained about not having their own parking spots. Jeremy couldn't believe it. These professional business people were worse than his apartment tenants!

Then Jeremy truly discovered that all that glitters is not gold. The economy entered a recession and businesses began to go under. To his shock and dismay, the unsinkable investment banking tenant was folding. In what felt like an instant, one of his main two tenants was gone; out of business and not paying him rent. Although it was prime class A space, businesses were tightening their belts to brace for the worst that the recession may dish out so finding a new tenant proved to be very difficult.

The attorney also dropped a bomb on Jeremy shortly thereafter that he was not going to renew the lease since the investment banking tenant was gone. Jeremy discovered that the attorney gathered some of his clients from the investment bank and in order for his legal practice to continue to thrive, he would need to move offices to another building where complimentary businesses could help feed his business. Jeremy never quite believed that reasoning because most attorneys don't build long standing operations based on the foot traffic from adjacent businesses. Nevertheless, the attorney would be leaving in 8 months and Jeremy would need to fill the space or else be left paying for the majority of the building on his own since the remaining tenants only represented a 20% occupancy.

The recession lasted for several more years. During that time, Jeremy never did get either of the two main spaces filled. He used every bit of positive cash flow from his other apartment building to cover the monthly obligations of the Icon. Even that was not enough though and soon, he began to fall behind on payments. He reached out to every bank in town for help and every single one was not interested in a 20% occupied office building during the midst of an economic downturn.

The widow eventually foreclosed and Jeremy lost the property and his $600,000 investment. It was a very sad ending to what had begun as such a crowning achievement in his investing life. And to add insult to injury, the apartment building he sold was still going strong, weathering the storm of the recession with ease. In fact, it was actually performing better than ever because misplaced homeowners due to their own foreclosures had driven them into apartments. Had he not purchased the Icon and held onto his apartment building, Jeremy would have been cash flowing better than ever.

Powerful and Profitable Learning Lessons

(1) All that glitters is not gold. Beautiful, class A buildings may not be as profitable investments as class B and C properties for the individual commercial real estate investor.

(2) Never fall in love with a property. Jeremy, years later in retrospect, said in an interview with the author that his biggest mistake was falling in love with the building. The fact was, the property he sold earned more money than the Icon. Rather than using the cold hard numbers to make the investment decision, he saw the marble and chandeliers in the lobby of the Icon versus laundry facilities and old barbeque grills in the common areas of the apartment property.

(3) Jeremy also discovered the ups and downs of real estate that rely on business tenants. When the economy is strong, filling office space vacancies is much easier than when the economy takes a nose dive. Whereas, with apartments, everyone needs a place to live.

6. The Extortionist Judge

Jim needed to buy several adjacent properties in order to complete the development he had planned. He meticulously negotiated purchase contracts with each of the property owners and proceeded to perform the due diligence on each of them. After the inspections and research were deemed satisfactory, Jim began to schedule the closings of each of the properties.

The most important tract was the back 8 acres owned by a local judge. Jim reached out to each seller to coordinate the closing and when he talked to the judge, the gentlemen asked to close last. Curious, Jim asked him why he wanted to close after every other property owner. The judge replied, "As a judge, I have presided over a lot of cases involving dishonest business practitioners and investors. Call me paranoid, or just not trusting, but I want to close last just in case you have something up your sleeve." Jim shrugged his shoulders and agreed to the judge's request.

After closing and purchasing all of the other properties, it was time to close on the judge's 8 acres. Jim got quite the surprise when the judge told him that he would only close if he got an additional $250,000. Jim retorted, "Are you out of your mind? We have a legally binding contract. This is extortion. I will sue for specific performance if you don't close and you know I will win!" To which the judge calmly responded, "By the time you get that victory through the justice system, it will be several years down the road. I know exactly what to do to ensure this case gets pushed off year after year. Meanwhile, you would have had to carry the property taxes and debt service on all those other properties for many years. Plus, by that time, the market may be completely different, your prospective tenants may not even be interested anymore and this development may be a complete flop. Paying me $250,000 more now is a whole lot cheaper than the alternative."

Jim begrudgingly agreed and gave the judge an additional $250,000 in cash.

Powerful and Profitable Learning Lessons

(1) Be very careful when doing deals with attorneys or judges. They know the legal system better than you do and can cause you all kinds of problems.

(2) Anytime a participant in a deal asks to change a seemingly innocuous term in the agreement, think long and hard as to why they are really doing it.

(3) If you are buying several adjacent properties, close them all on the same day to prevent the last one from extorting you. Or, follow in Walt Disney's footsteps and buy each property in different purchaser names as to not alert anyone that it is the same organization buying all of the properties.

Phil Pustejovsky

7. Cash at Closing

Just prior to closing, a seller of a $2M property was looking to back out because he found out he could get $2.3M from another buyer. He thought he had come up with an ingenious loophole to stop the closing. The contract stated that the seller was to receive cash at closing. So on the day of closing, he demanded the title company pay him in cash. He said he wouldn't sign the papers if he didn't get cash. He wouldn't accept a wire transfer or a cashier's check.

The buyer, Ben, and the title company were both furious. And with only one day left until the contract date expired, Ben had to come up with a solution fast or he would lose this incredible deal. He called up his banker and asked how quickly he could get his hands on $2M in cash. Ben's banker was puzzled as to why they couldn't just send a wire, but Ben quickly caught the banker up to speed as to what the seller was doing. After a quick exchange of ideas, Ben came up with a plan to not only meet the seller's demands, but also get that seller back for creating such a hassle.

Ben informed the title company that he could perform on the seller's request and said he would have $2M in cash tomorrow. That night, an armored car drove $2M to the location of the closing company. Then, an hour before the closing, Ben met the armored car outside the title company and the cash was brought into the title office. Next, the title agent counted up all the cash and verified it was the correct amount. Then, together both the title agent and Ben proceeded to tear off the paper sleeves that bound the cash together and placed the loose bills on the closing table in a huge pile.

The title company had the seller sign and then led him back to the room that housed the cash he demanded. What the seller discovered was two million $1 bills loosely piled up on a closing table. It was then up to him to count it as well as transport it out of the closing office and eventually either deposit it in his bank or stuff it under his mattress.

Powerful and Profitable Learning Lessons

(1) Make sure your purchase contract specifies that the funds to the seller can be in the form of cash, cashier's check, or wire.

(2) Don't assume a deal is going to close until the seller has signed the closing papers and the money has transferred to the appropriate parties.

Phil Pustejovsky

8. $375,000 Cash Tied Up in a Legal Quagmire

Years of attempts to negotiate a short sale had come to this; a foreclosure auction scheduled for the next day. Sam, the investor who had been valiantly working the file, was on the phone with the borrower, Henry, and his foreclosure defense attorney to finalize the plan for the next day. Henry made it clear, "Sam, if you can get the property at a price you like at the auction tomorrow, my attorney won't file anything to try to reverse the foreclosure sale. But, if you don't buy it, then we're going to attempt to file something that could possibly reverse the foreclosure sale." Henry's attorney agreed and it appeared everyone was on the same page.

Sam had been around the block and had seen some pretty remarkable moves foreclosure defense attorneys had done to *postpone* a foreclosure. But, in his entire career, he had never heard of a foreclosure sale being reversed *after* the auction. Once the proverbial gavel had been dropped, in all cases, in his experience, it was the point of no return. Sam didn't give the borrower or his attorney another thought, but instead, focused his mental energy on the maximum amount he would be comfortable with bidding.

Sam was in a far superior position to any other foreclosure auction bidder on the day of the sale. Since he had been working a short sale on the property prior to the foreclosure, he had conducted a recent appraisal and an inspection. So unlike everyone else who would be bidding "as is and sight unseen," Sam knew exactly what he was getting himself into before he showed up.

The bidding began and the only bidders were himself and a representative of the bank who wanted to ensure the bank at least got their reserve amount. In increments of $1,000, the bid began to climb. Sam had planned to not go above $375,000 and fortunately (or unfortunately), the bank representative ended his bidding at $374,000 so Sam got the property literally at the exact highest amount he was willing to pay for it. It was almost eerie how it had happened that way.

Sam scurried to a local bank branch and got a cashier's check for the balance due. Upon handing the money to the foreclosure auction processor, he noticed that he didn't get the title to the property immediately. Curious, he asked what the holdup was, since he thought at the point the money was paid, the property became his. The government worker replied, "In this state, there is a 7 day period whereby if the foreclosure auction is contested, you may not become the owner, but instead, your money would be returned to you." Immediately upon learning of this, he dialed Henry to let him know that he had won the auction for an amount he was comfortable with and based on yesterday's conversation, that meant the deal was done. Henry thanked Sam for all he had done to try to get a short sale done and was glad to see Sam was being rewarded for all that effort by getting the property for the amount he wanted.

On the 7th day, Sam inquired about next steps on finalizing his ownership of the property and to his surprise, the file showed that a formal document had been filed by the borrower to contest the foreclosure. Therefore, Sam would not be getting the title to the property that day.

Sam felt betrayed. He immediately called Henry demanding an explanation and all Henry could offer him is that he had changed his mind and that he and his attorney felt that Sam had gotten the property too cheap. Sam was furious.

Back on the phone with the foreclosure office, he asked, "Well, I guess if I am not going to get this property, I'm going to get a refund of the $375,000 cash I paid you. Can I get that today?" To which the response came back, "No. In order to get a refund, it has be ordered by the judge. These situations are very rare but it could be several months before that happens, if not longer."

Not only had Sam NOT become the owner of that property for the purchase price of $375,000, but also, that amount was now in the custody of the local government and there was no time frame on when it was coming back!

In panic mode, Sam reached out to several other foreclosure attorneys to make some sense of the matter. And to his horror, they all responded that it was one of the many risks in buying at a foreclosure auction, and furthermore that they never advised their clients to buy at a foreclosure auction for this and many other reasons. And just when he thought it couldn't get any worse, he discovered that the local government was short on judges and foreclosure cases were backed up for months. In fact, a judge from another part of the state had been hired to help with the backlog but she was on a one month leave of absence!

After 6 months of effort, a judge finally gave the order to refund Sam's money. But they made some paperwork mistakes which held it up another month. On the 7th month, the money was returned. No interest. No apologies. No recouping of the opportunity costs for not having that capital available to do other deals. Meanwhile, the borrower regained ownership and through a legal loophole, still owns that property today, even though the mortgage is not being paid.

Powerful and Profitable Learning Lessons

(1) Buyers and sellers change their minds, often.

(2) Only bid on properties at a foreclosure auction if you completely understand all the laws, procedures and risks.

Phil Pustejovsky

9. Making the Seller Your Partner

A prime tract of land had been owned by a local farmer and upon the old farmer's passing, had been inherited by his daughter, Lisa. The land became incredibly valuable because an interstate interchange had been constructed and several class A office buildings and hotels had been developed nearby.

An enterprising commercial real estate agent, Brian, noticed this tract of raw land and tracked down the new owner. Brian attempted to purchase the land outright from Lisa but she did her research and discovered that some raw land owners could negotiate a partnership with the developer rather than a cash sale. The property was so good that Brian agreed to a 50/50 partnership despite knowing very little about Lisa.

Brian used the skills he had acquired over a lifetime of experience to create a Planned Urban Development (PUD) and get it approved by the city. It took about one year and nearly $400,000 to pull it off, but in the end, the entire tract of land had been segmented for different uses, from apartments to retail. Lisa didn't have the money to cover the property tax bill, so Brian paid for that too, in addition to all the costs to originate the PUD. Before Brian had met Lisa, the land had raw opportunity, but couldn't reach its full potential. After Brian's magic touches, the land could maximize its earning potential.

The partnership was arranged under the plan for Brian to fully develop the property, complete with a shopping center, luxury apartment complex and outparcels for single building tenants like a bank or chain restaurant. But once the PUD was completed and approved, Brian saw that he and Lisa could make great money just selling off the parcels. They sold one parcel and both pocketed $500,000 each! That was just the beginning, thought Brian.

Then, Brian got a rude awakening when a lawsuit appeared on his desk. Lisa was suing him for not developing the property as was originally agreed. Brian realized that the thank you he got for helping Lisa earn $500,000 from their partnership, was a lawsuit funded by that money! Lisa's goal was simple; get rid of Brian.

The case dragged on for years, but in the end, Brian lost and was removed from the deal. One month after Lisa had become 100% owner in the deal, she sold the remaining parcels to a developer for $10M.

Powerful and Profitable Learning Lessons

(1) Don't make the seller your partner.

(2) Always build in the ability for multiple options in a deal because you never know what the future holds and locking yourself into only one exit strategy in a deal from the onset greatly limits your profit potential.

Phil Pustejovsky

10. Ignoring Commitments Made in Writing

When the real estate market tanked, one of the most effective strategies for getting a great deal on a property was to negotiate a short sale with the seller's lender. In a short sale, the bank agrees to accept an amount that is less than their full payoff. Mortgage companies agree to a short sale because they can sometimes make out better in the end than having to foreclose on the property.

As any borrower has experienced, when a mortgage is originated, there is a large number of documents that must be signed. Naturally, when a short sale is being approved, the bank also requires some documents to be signed. One of those documents that some banks require a buyer sign is an affidavit that stipulates that the buyer agrees not to resell the property for 90 days from the date of purchase.

"What does the bank care and what would they do anyways if they found out that the property was sold in less than 90 days?" thought Randy and Roger as they read over the affidavit that the bank required they sign at the short sale closing. Further, they became convinced that a lien holder for a seller didn't have the right to dictate what a new buyer could do with an asset once they owned it, so Randy and Roger proceeded with their plan to resell the property a few weeks later to a new buyer for more money.

It took some real maneuvering to make it work because they had to use two different closing companies and they had to make sure the new title company was unaware of the affidavits they were signing which committed them to holding onto the property for 90 days or more. Plus, they used elaborate ownership structures to change who they thought could be considered the actual owner, thereby absolving themselves of the affidavit commitment.

And after they had done it once with no problems, they did it again, and again and again.

Over the course of two years, the tandem tallied up 20 short sale closings whereby they had resold the properties to new buyers within less than 90 days.

But, on the 21st deal, things began to change. The agent for the new title company had experience with short sales and was perplexed by how Randy and Roger were able to resell the property in less than 90 days. She saw on the deed the name of the individual who had drafted the document and contacted her to inquire about this closing that had occurred about a month prior. As she suspected, the previous closing agent confirmed that the bank had required Randy and Roger to sign an affidavit committing them to not sell the property for 90 days. The title agent kindly explained to Randy and Roger that they were restricted from reselling for 90 days and that she couldn't close this until day 91. Undeterred, they went looking for another closing firm that was not quite as bright.

Meanwhile, the buyers were having difficulty getting the loan due to the limited size of their down payment. Randy and Roger came up with a plan. They would give the buyer the down payment on the day of closing in the form of a cashier's check from their bank account but with the buyer's name on it. It wasn't going to cost them any money because as soon as they gave the buyer the money, it would come right back to them.

They executed the plan to perfection and closed with a new title company. Randy and Roger had been on a roll for over 2 years now and calculated that they had brought in over $500,000 in net profits. Patting themselves on the back, they considered themselves geniuses for having gotten around problems that other investors couldn't.

Unfortunately, the buyers on the 21st deal began to run into financial issues a few months after closing on the property. They were struggling to make the mortgage payments so they applied for a loan modification. Their mortgage company poured over the documents the borrowers sent in the loan modification package and began to see discrepancies with the original loan application when they bought the home. That spurned on further investigations, including discovering the peculiar cashier's check at the closing that didn't seem to come from any of the borrowers' bank accounts.

By accepting the down payment from the sellers Randy and Roger, the borrowers had committed loan fraud. But rather than go after these struggling homeowners, the bank identified a larger target; Randy and Roger.

With nearly unlimited funds to pay for legal investigations, the bank set their sights on the duo that had sold the property to the sellers and the investigators soon discovered that they may have struck gold. Not only had the Randy and Roger conspired to commit mortgage fraud by giving the borrowers the down payment on the day of closing, but far more serious was that they had signed affidavits confirming that they wouldn't sell the property in less than 90 days and yet they had done so anyways.

Randy and Roger were indicted. Rather than fight a very long and costly legal battle, Randy and Roger both pled guilty.

Today, they are behind bars and hoping through more work with their attorney, for a reduced sentence.

Powerful and Profitable Learning Lessons

(1) Don't commit mortgage fraud, ever.

(2) Before you sign paperwork, especially with banks, understand the legal ramifications of ignoring the commitments you make in writing.

Phil Pustejovsky

11. The Wrong Way to Lend Money on Real Estate

Dr. Simmons had worked hard for many years to finally have a medical practice of his own and his efforts were beginning to pay off. He had always wanted to invest in real estate on the side too and he heard about a monthly meeting whereby local real estate investors got together to network and share ideas. The doctor thought this could be an ideal place to learn more about real estate investing and meet the right people to help him get started with it. Wandering about the room, a very professional and kind older gentleman struck up a conversation with him.

John seemed like a very seasoned investor with the kind of financial life Dr. Simmons was looking to attain one day. John summarized his life story, from how he transitioned from working in a plant and renovating houses on the side to making the leap to full time real estate investor and later, representing Japanese buyers to help buy hotels. Now with his $4M portfolio of rental properties, he was taking it easy, living the good life and just doing a few deals here and there to keep from getting too bored. They swapped business cards and each went onto network with others that night.

The next month, the doctor ran into John again and they resumed their previous conversation. John had just located a great deal and was shopping hard money lenders to see who could give him the best rate that night. John had explained that even though he had the money, his personal rule was to always use OPM (other people's money) whenever possible. Dr. Simmons was curious as to the rates that hard money lenders got and was blown away when 13%-15% per year plus a few percentage points upon origination was customary. Immediately, the doctor offered to be the hard money lender since he was getting far lower rates of return where his money was currently sitting at a brokerage house. John explained that Larry, on the other side of the room, would do it for 2% upfront plus 13% per year and so the doctor offered 2% upfront and 12% per year. They shook on it and the doctor went home beaming with excitement to get a chance at his first deal.

The loan paperwork was handled by a closing attorney and the process went smoothly. After closing, John went to work on fixing up the house and then listed it for sale. It sold quite quickly and about 3 months from the date the loan was originated, the doctor was headed to the closing office to pick up his check for the loan payback plus his interest.

As the doctor was walking out of the office, elated at how easy that deal was and how well it went, he asked John if there were any more deals like this. John said, "As a matter of fact, I do have another one that I could use your help on." And while still at the closing attorney's office, they had new loan paperwork drawn up and signed and the doctor signed his check over to John. Simmons thought he had made quite an intelligent move. His money was being put back to work for him without a day's rest.

The problem was that the second lending deal happened so fast that Dr. Simmons didn't take the time to think through an extremely important part of lending money on real estate...the position of the loan. Unlike the first deal, whereby his money was protected by a mortgage in the first position, in this second deal, there was already an existing first mortgage on the property so his loan had to be subordinated, or put in an inferior position behind the first mortgage.

Unfortunately, this second loan to John did not get paid off quite as quickly. And as the months wore on, John continued to make more and more excuses. He explained that he had a buyer for his $4M portfolio and the cash from that would pay off the doctor's loan. Eventually, John stopped attending the local investment meetings and he wasn't responding to Dr. Simmons correspondence. With no other options, the doctor hired a foreclosure attorney to foreclose on John.

Once the attorney got involved, Dr. Simmons discovered some discouraging information. First, the loan wasn't against an investment property at all, but was actually recorded against John's primary residence. Second, and far more problematic, was that John had actually originated another private money loan with another person he had met at that investor club meeting a few days prior and it got recorded before the doctor's lien. Since it all happened so fast the day the loan was made, there was no title search done so the doctor really had no idea what other liens were against the property and he didn't purchase title insurance to protect himself in case of title problems like this. When it was finally discovered, the end result was that Dr. Simmons had a $100,000 third mortgage behind a $150,000 first mortgage and a $50,000 second mortgage on a house worth about $150,000. In other words, the doctor's lien was basically unprotected.

Without the collateral from the real estate to protect his money, Simmons thought at least he could pursue John personally since he thought John had significant assets in which to go after. He learned that John had a $4M rental portfolio with $4.5M in loans against it. John was beyond broke.

In the end, Dr. Simmons never recovered his original investment and with the additional attorney's fees, it ended up being a huge loss for him. In turns out, John had swindled quite a few people from that local investor club. John never did get in any legal trouble although he created several personal enemies. The stress of having screwed a bunch of people out of money eventually got the best of John. He died of a heart attack. He certainly left behind good lessons in what NOT to do when lending money to another person for real estate investing.

Powerful and Profitable Learning Lessons

(1) Always do a title search and get a lender's title insurance policy when lending money on real estate.

(2) Always understand the many different facets of a deal, from the value, to the work required to renovate, to the market conditions, thoroughly before lending money on real estate.

(3) Verify what a borrower tells you before you lend.

(4) Have an attorney on your side prior to funding the deal to make sure you didn't miss any details that could render your investment vulnerable.

Phil Pustejovsky

12. When It Rains, It Pours

Kurt had been laid off due to his company going bankrupt and worst of all, the pension he had been counting on for retirement was gone too. But, unlike many of his older co-workers, he still had time to do something about his future nest egg. After he secured another job, rather than count on a company for his long term financial security, he took matters into his own hands and began learning about real estate investing.

The plan Kurt came up with involved buying new built homes on 15 year mortgages and renting them out. About the time of his retirement, his goal was to have 6 houses owned free and clear (without a mortgage) and the rental income would be his retirement income. Rather than diversifying his portfolio across different locations, Kurt wanted to keep his property management simple by owning all the units in the same area. Therefore, Kurt ended up purchasing 6 new homes in a newly constructed subdivision over the course of two years.

Like any landlord, he had his ups and downs with tenants but he managed to stay the course by not selling any of his houses, despite being very tempted to several times. Eventually, he paid all 6 mortgages off completely and had achieved his retirement goal.

About that time, a thunderstorm rumbled through one early summer afternoon, bringing with it lightning and plenty of rain. But unlike every other rain storm that anyone could recall experiencing, this storm stuck around for several days. And the heavy rains continued. After 4 days, the water began to collect in low lying areas and the first signs of flooding were evident.

Meteorologists could see what was happening but couldn't explain why this intense rain storm wouldn't move off to the east like every storm had done in their experience. The 500 year flood zone areas on FEMA maps were beginning to experience flooding and thousands of houses began to see water filling up their crawl spaces and basements.

The Army Corps of Engineers had built a dam on one corner of the big lake in town but didn't calculate for such a freak of nature as this storm. The water level eventually rose beyond the height of the dam and water began to spill over adding even more water to the already flooded river on the other side of the dam. The news alerted everyone downstream of the dam to evacuate because if the dam broke, then it could be catastrophic.

Kurt's nest egg of houses was situated in a subdivision downstream of that dam. Although not in a flood zone, his properties were still in close proximity to the river that was now overflowing from the excess water spilling over the dam. His tenants had safely evacuated and all he could do was stay glued to the news and watch the events unfold.

He thought he caught a break when the rains stopped, the dam did not break and the flood waters began to reside. Once the roadways in that area were navigable, he rushed over to see just how high the water rose. It was worse than he thought. Water had reached the second floor of all his properties. They were destroyed and would need to be torn down.

His hazard insurance policy excluded flood damage so he didn't get any help from the property insurance he had been faithfully paying on for over 16 years. The federal government organization FEMA came in and helped many homeowners whose home insurance had refused to pay out claims. They didn't extend any help to Kurt though because rental properties were excluded from relief.

After weighing his options, he put his now 6 vacant lots up for sale and eventually sold them for next to nothing.

This very sad story does have some tremendously valuable lessons.

Powerful and Profitable Learning Lessons

(1) Floods do occur, even in non-flood zone areas. In fact, flooding is surprisingly more common near rivers, lakes and oceans than most people think. Therefore, strongly consider purchasing flood insurance for properties you own near water or other low lying areas.

(2) Diversify your rental portfolio. Although owning in the same geographic region is advisable for many reasons (laws, location of your team, etc), compiling your entire collection propertics within the exact same subdivision can expose you to problems. A flood or a tornado, for example, typically affects certain parts of a region more than others and spreading out your holdings across different parts of a geographic area can help protect you from natural disasters wiping out everything you own. But also, especially over the long term, certain areas of town do better than others and sometimes it can be hard to predict. What today might be a booming area might tomorrow be a bad part of town. And, what might be a marginal area today might turn into the hottest and most desirable place to live years later.

13. Sale and Leaseback

Kim was losing her home to foreclosure. It was a sad ending to an already tragic situation. She had lost her husband to cancer and the lack of income along with all the bills had forced her to fall behind on mortgage payments, unable to catch up on past due payments. On fixed income, she could afford the monthly payment, but she had no way of bringing the loan current. Month after month, she received frightening foreclosure letters and Kim was running out of options.

About two months before the property was scheduled to go to auction, Kim reached out to a close friend and proposed an idea. "What if I sell the house to you, you buy it, and then I rent the house back from you?" Sally knew Kim's situation and it seemed like a reasonable solution to the problem because Kim did have consistent fixed income coming in that could easily afford the monthly payment. Without much time to fully explore the ramifications of the decision, Sally moved forward with the idea, obtained a loan, purchased the property and Kim remained in the property as the tenant.

Only a few months into this new arrangement, Sally began noticing that her monthly rent payments began to arrive later and later. For someone on fixed income, Kim should have sent them on the same day each month. At first Sally didn't think too much about it until Kim became more and more difficult to reach by phone when the rent was due. Sally went so far as to knock on the door to make sure that there was nothing medically wrong and she was shocked to discover that Kim was simply ignoring her.

Soon, the rent payments from Kim stopped coming. Not only had the personal relationship they had had together for decades deteriorated in a matter of months, but also, Sally was now having to juggle two house payments in order to save her own credit. Sally wasn't a rich person and eventually she had to fall behind on the mortgage payments of the house Kim was living in. She reached out to a real estate investor to possibly purchase the house and was told that the non-paying tenant would need to be evicted first before they would buy it.

Sally was still a bit in shock over how this whole situation had gone down when she contacted an eviction attorney. As if things couldn't get any worse, the attorney informed Sally that evicting Kim could be extremely difficult since she had formerly been the homeowner. The law was definitely on Kim's side. In fact, it could have been argued that Sally had committed equity skimming by purchasing Kim's house while in foreclosure without the proper disclosures and was now trying to finish off the scam by evicting Kim!

Sally was dumbfounded. Instead of being praised for helping Kim at a time when absolutely no one else would, she was potentially being punished for it. Sally now knew what it felt like when a rescuer tries to save a drowning person only to experience the victim drowning the rescuer.

Sally had no choice but to move through the legal process of eviction because she couldn't continue to have the property occupied by a non-paying tenant. Kim ignored all attempts at correspondence and Sally prayed that the legal system would eventually land in her favor.

Kim found free, quality legal representation from the local Legal Aid office and with their help, the case lingered on for years while Kim was able to live rent free. Eventually, several years later, the eviction court judge determined that it was not a "Tenant-Landlord" case, but instead, as a business transaction, and would have to go before the local Supreme Court.

Before it could ever make it to the local Supreme Court though, the property was foreclosed upon by the bank. It had been years of accumulated unpaid mortgage payments so the total payoff far exceeded the current value of the property and at the foreclosure auction, the final amount it went to auction for was much less than the total mortgage balance. This created a large deficit which Sally now owed the bank. Sally had no choice but to file bankruptcy and lose her own home in the process.

Powerful and Profitable Learning Lessons

(1) Don't buy properties from struggling homeowners and then lease the property back to them. Although the "Sale and Leaseback" is common in commercial real estate, it is a completely different transaction when dealing with homeowners. The likelihood that someone who couldn't or wouldn't pay their mortgage company in the past, will be more likely to pay a landlord like you in the future, is slim to none. If you are going to buy properties in foreclosure from defaulted borrowers, they must move out and find another place to live.

(2) Sally is actually fortunate she didn't get into any criminal trouble over what she did. Some investors have actually gone to jail over doing this. Recently, laws have been enacted to protect homeowners who are far behind on payments. If you're going to purchase a property from someone who is in foreclosure, make sure you understand the laws protecting that borrower to ensure you don't participate in any unintended criminal activity. Be very careful!

(3) Avoid making your friends, your tenants. That will also oftentimes end badly. Not "if," but "when" they don't pay you, not only will the friendship be over, but also your friend will probably put up more of a legal fight than someone you never knew before they rented your property.

14. Insurance Exclusions

Jill was so excited to purchase her first home. Only a few years out of nursing school, she had a great job at the local hospital and was ready to take the next step in her life of becoming a homeowner. Although she didn't have the entire down payment, her parents chipped in for the rest of what was needed because they saw their little daughter maturing into a wonderful, independent woman and wanted to support her in this endeavor.

After a few years, she fell in love with a gentlemen in medical school and his residency took him 1,000 miles away. Rather than try to manage a long distance relationship, she decided to follow him. Although she felt he was "the one," she didn't know how it would all work out. So, rather than sell her home, she put it up for rent. It rented almost immediately.

Jill had never been a landlord so she hired a property management firm to handle everything for her. And for 8 months, all was well, because the only task she had to complete was to deposit the check that was mailed to her from the property manager each month. And then, she got the call from the manager that changed everything.

The tenants had clogged the upstairs toilet, it had overflowed, and it had continued to overflow for more than a day. By the time the tenants stopped the flooding, water had damaged the two bedrooms and bathroom upstairs and then the water had continued its destruction downstairs, ruining the ceiling in many places and the flooring pretty much throughout. Drywall, baseboards, sub flooring, carpet, wood flooring, and much more would have to be replaced. The remediation process would take weeks when it was all said and done.

Jill filed a claim with her insurance company. Unfortunately, she had the wrong coverage in place. She had never changed her policy to a landlord policy. Instead, the insurance was still written as if Jill lived in the property and it was her primary residence. Jill got introduced to the concept of insurance exclusions. The entire debacle was not covered by her insurance. She would be on her own to pay for the fix up.

Although her parents had helped her with the down payment, they were not in a financial position to help her now. Her new boyfriend was barely getting by since he was not yet a medical doctor so he couldn't help either. She had to borrow anywhere and everywhere she could to come up with the money.

Once the work was finished, she put the property up for sale and after commissions and closing costs, the proceeds from the sale just about covered the remediation costs. She didn't get her down payment back and she didn't receive any financial benefit from the appreciation the house experienced over those several years. In the end, the mistake of not changing over her insurance policy to a landlord policy cost her all the financial benefits of being a homeowner during that time.

Powerful and Profitable Learning Lessons

(1) Make sure your insurance coverages on your real estate is correct at all times, especially if you make ownership or occupancy changes.

(2) Whether you own 1 or 100 properties, it is your responsibility as the owner to have the correct insurance in place.

Phil Pustejovsky

15. They're Not Making Any More of It

Glenn had heard from his father say over and over growing up the phrase, "Land, they're not making any more of it." Although his father never had any money to invest, he sometimes talked about land as being the best investment. Once Glenn reached the age where saving and investing became important to him, he remembered his father's affinity for land and began to study how to best invest in it.

Glenn stumbled upon a concept for acquiring land at potentially pennies on the dollar by paying for another property owner's taxes, often referred to as tax lien investing. When property owners fell behind on their taxes, the local governmental authority responsible for collecting those taxes would do something quite unique. Rather than hire a collections law firm to get the money from the past due owners, the government would ask investors to pay the tax bills on behalf of the owner. In exchange, the investor would get a certificate guaranteeing a significant interest rate on their money and the ability to become the land owner if they weren't paid back within a few years.

What was most appealing to Glenn was that there was a chance to actually own the land in the event the property owner never paid back the tax lien. Sure, the guaranteed interest rate was nice, but after attending a few tax lien sales, he noticed that oftentimes the interest rates were bid down significantly by the other investors competing against each other. He wanted to own some land because "they weren't making any more it."

Without much money to work with, and being that tax lien investing was a cash sport, Glenn sat through a few tax lien sales to get a feel for the process. It took him quite a bit of time to work up the courage to actually bid on his first tax lien. The public records information stated that it was a small vacant lot with a tax assessment value of $9,638 and the cost of the tax lien was $2,783. This was one of the lowest priced tax liens for sale that day too. Glenn had worked very hard to save up $3,000; almost two years, so this represented all the money in the world to him. It was no longer an idea though. It was real now. He took a deep breath and raised his hand to indicate he was bidding. Unlike most of the other tax liens, there were no other bidders and in a few seconds, he was the winner!

Relief and excitement swept over Glenn as he walked to the front of the room to get his certificate. He transferred the money to the county tax collector and went home the proud new owner of a tax lien certificate. It gave him comfort knowing that he had a guaranteed interest rate and the worst thing that could happen is that the property owner would fail to pay him back and then he would become the new owner of the property, which is what he ultimately wanted anyways. This was especially true considering the value was nearly $10,000 and he paid less than $3,000 for it.

He instantly wanted to do more but he didn't have any money. So he went back to the daily grind of trying to save a few bucks here and there in hopes of buying another tax lien sometime down the road. But, like so many others, life got in the way of his ability to save. Unexpected bills, car troubles, medical deductibles, and old appliances seemed to always deplete the meager amount he managed to save. Before long, it had been two years and to his pleasant surprise, Glenn's tax lien had matured without being paid back and therefore he could possibly become the owner.

In order for Glenn to officially become the owner, first, the property would go to a tax deed sale whereby the auction would start with an opening bid of the full amount owed to Glenn. Then, if no one else bid on the property, Glenn would win the tax deed sale by default and become the owner. That's exactly what happened. Although several properties were auctioned off at the tax deed sale to other buyers, no one bid more than the amount owed to Glenn so he officially became the owner of the property. Glenn thought he had hit the jackpot!

The property turned out to be a very odd shaped sliver of land on a busy road. Glenn did some research with the city building department and learned that it was far too small to ever have anything built on it, especially with how thin it was which would not allow for the minimum setbacks the building codes stipulated. Although disappointed, Glenn continued to strategize how his land could pay him dividends.

The idea of putting a billboard on the property seemed plausible. He contacted the sign ordinance department and learned that due to its location, no sign could be constructed on the land either.

Then, Glenn got his first unpleasant experience with being a land owner. He got a tax bill. And it reminded him of how he got the property in the first place. The previous owner didn't pay his tax bills and lost the property.

A few months went by and then Glenn got a letter from the Codes Department with a violation fine for not removing the trash from his land. He thought it was a mistake! Trash? What trash? So, Glenn took a drive over to his little sliver of land to see what was going on and low and behold, it had a bunch of trash on it. A strange phenomenon was occurring whereby his little lot made for an easy place for people to pull in and dump their trash. The grass was waist high too. So, he went back home, got his lawn mower, work gloves, and trash bags and then spent the rest of that day cleaning up his property. He then sent a check to pay the codes violation fine.

All of a sudden, his land investment wasn't quite as profitable as he had initially envisioned. Not only did he have a yearly tax bill, but he also had to maintain the property periodically to avoid fines from the city. Glenn decided the best way to make the most of this deal would be to sell it because after all, the value was at least $10,000.

He couldn't find a real estate agent willing to take the time to list it because the price was too low and their commission would be too small to make it worth their time. He put a For Sale by Owner sign on the property. He got a few calls now and again but each time, once it was discovered that the shape of the lot didn't allow for building a new structure and the location did not allow for a billboard, the prospective buyer lost interest.

About a year later, the property next door sold to a new owner and that person expressed interest in buying Glenn's little parcel. After much disappointment, this was the first true glimmer of hope Glenn had felt for this property since he first got it. The prospective buyer asked Glenn to do a title search and that's when Glenn discovered yet another wrinkle. In order to obtain clear title from a property acquired through a tax lien, he had to file a legal process called Quiet Title. It would cost nearly $2,000 in legal fees to complete, and potentially more since he hadn't initiated the process years before when he should have. Glenn didn't have the money and it didn't seem to be worth it at this point anyways based on the tiny amount the new buyer was thinking of paying.

Glenn pondered over the situation. He had basically spent his meager life savings for the privilege of having to pay taxes each year on a property that he would also have to consistently require the removal of trash and the mowing of the grass. There was only one potential buyer, the next door neighbor, but even he wasn't willing to pay anywhere near what the tax department assessed the value at. Plus, in order to be able to sell it, he would have to pay thousands more in legal fees.

That's when he began to put some pieces together in his mind. Perhaps no one else bid on the tax lien for this property because they knew something he didn't about the property? Perhaps, again, no other investors bid at the tax deed sale for this property because they recognized the potential pitfalls? Most importantly, maybe the previous owner of this lot purposely didn't pay the taxes and let the city take it from him to avoid the ongoing expenses?

In the end, Glenn got tired of maintaining the property and paying the taxes so he intentionally let the tax bills go unpaid. Eventually, the tax lien sale occurred with no bidders and in the end, the city became the owner of the property.

Powerful and Profitable Learning Lessons

(1) Yes, it is possible to go wrong buying land. They may not "be making any more of it" but that is not reason enough alone to buy it.

(2) The value assessed by the government for property tax calculation purposes usually does not accurately describe the true market value.

(3) Before ever bidding on and buying a tax lien certificate, you should know the underlying property very well, because one day, you may end up becoming the owner of it.

(4) If you are going to enter the realm of tax lien certificates and tax deed sales, you must understand the laws surrounding how you can get clear title if you do end up with the property. Every area is very different so you must get competent legal help for your specific area.

16. The FBI is Investigating You

Cindy was about to collect nearly $18,000 on her very first deal. Using some creative investing savvy, she had located a buyer for a property that the current owner had struggled to sell. This new buyer was represented by a real estate agent and he was pre-approved for a new loan.

Since Cindy had not been the owner of record on title for an extended period of time, the new buyer's mortgage loan originator was having difficulty getting underwriting approval. Cindy offered to have her go-to mortgage person, who was proficient at originating no title seasoning loans, to originate the loan for the buyer. A seemingly innocent proposal to the new buyer's agent created a result she would have never expected.

She got a call back from the real estate agent representing the new buyer the next day and the person proceeded to tell her, "I don't know if I should tell you this, but I feel you have a right to know. My broker just told me that he heard that you are being investigated by the FBI for your involvement in this deal. I guess they are cracking down on real estate flippers like you in this state."

Cindy thought to herself, "Oh my goodness, the FBI? Real estate flipping is being investigated in this state?" She proceeded to panic, her fears began to drift her mind into her worst nightmares. This was the last thing she had ever wanted from getting into real estate. Her original plan was to make enough money to finally quit her job and have some freedom. Instead, on her very first deal, it could land her in legal bondage!

In trying to regain her composure, she asked the agent, "What should I do? I don't want any trouble."

Calmly, the agent replied, "I don't know how much you're making, but I suppose it's probably not worth what the FBI could do to you."

Immediately, Cindy went to work on how to remove herself from this deal. Fortunately for her, she was in the Freedom Mentor Apprentice Program and once she shared this change of events to one of our mentors, our team went to work on finding out what was really going on since it was clear that her actions were completely legal.

Here's what we discovered: First, the mortgage broker was the real estate agent's broker's wife. By Cindy suggesting that the new buyer use a different mortgage loan originator, that would take money away from the broker's wife even though she couldn't get the borrower a loan. Second, the original sellers had gotten greedy and rather than be happy that Cindy was getting their house sold for the amount they wanted, the sellers wanted to sabotage the $18,000 profit Cindy was making and try to keep it for themselves. So they had contacted the new buyer's real estate agent's broker for ideas on how to get rid of Cindy.

What this broker came up with is a classic way to extricate someone from a deal. Rather than try to push them out, you create a way in which they really want to leave. In this case, he made up this tall tale of an FBI investigation to scare Cindy into begging to leave the deal. To further solidify the muse, the broker also told the new buyers that Cindy was being investigated by the FBI, enhancing the seller's confidence in the efficacy of cutting Cindy out of the deal. The broker's plan would have worked had Cindy been on her own.

The broker's otherwise brilliant plan was foiled when our team instructed Cindy to call the new buyers directly by dialing the phone number on their earnest money deposit check. Early in the conversation, the new buyers learned that Cindy was the reason this whole deal had come together in the first place and that she had a solution to their loan problem. The new buyers just wanted to buy the home. They didn't care which mortgage loan originator got them the loan and they certainly didn't care that Cindy was making $18,000. Cindy explained that the buyer's agent's broker and his wife were holding up the deal because they didn't want to lose the mortgage loan origination fees.

Directly after the call with the new buyers, things changed dramatically. There was never another mention of the FBI. Within a few weeks, Cindy's go-to mortgage person had gotten the new buyers a loan and the deal closed with Cindy making the $18,000 she had earned.

Powerful and Profitable Learning Lessons

(1) Be in direct contact with buyers and sellers. When there are agents in the middle, things can fall apart.

(2) When you're the "middle man", there are usually other parties in the deal that want nothing more than to get rid of you. You must know you're stuff and be able to stand your ground when the inevitable threats come.

17. The Condo Association

Development was booming in this ocean front city. High rise condos were sprouting up like weeds and Lance wanted to get in on the wave of growth. The idea of investing in a condo appealed to him because he wouldn't have to ever deal with mowing grass, maintaining a pool, roof problems, or literally any other exterior problem whatsoever because the Condo Association would take care it. His plan was to buy, rent, and watch the appreciation climb. He anticipated that his net worth would skyrocket.

Lance did his homework on prices of condos around town and found a condo building that had a low monthly association payment of $100 and the prices were low in comparison to what he could rent it for. After he closed, he was able to find a tenant right away. But then, he had his first run in with the Condo Association as they required his tenant to be approved in order to rent in the building. Lance obviously didn't do his homework when it came to the bi-laws of the Association itself. Thankfully his first tenant was approved and he was now a landlord. His plan was coming together.

The cash flow after all expenses was not very much but Lance reasoned that in a few years, the value of the property would catapult upwards and therefore his real profit would come from the appreciation, not the cash flow. He was one of many speculators doing the same thing and he knew several people doing it too.

Like clockwork, prices of similar condos did rise and Lance even considered selling after just one year, but held back and renewed the lease with the tenant to hopefully capture another year of gains. Not a month after renewing the lease, he got a letter from the Condo Association about an assessment of $8,000 that every unit owner would be responsible for to replace the roof, fix the pool and perform several other significant repairs which were going to greatly exceed the available reserves the Association had built up. Lance thought it was a prank at first. Certainly this couldn't be true, he thought. How could they even have the authority to levy such a bill?

Lance did his research and discovered that the Condo Association had the power to do this. Lance didn't have the extra money available to pay them so eventually the Association recorded a lien against his property. But that's not all, they also initiated foreclosure proceedings. Lance ignored it, thinking that Condo Associations didn't have the power to do that.

Even though Lance continued to pay the monthly association dues on time and his mortgage too, he was still in foreclosure. When Lance finally woke up to the reality of the situation, he was unable to scrap up the money to pay off the lien and stop the foreclosure. It went to auction whereby someone paid the association lien amount and in exchange, became the owner.

Lance was so confused. How could someone else become the owner of the property when the first mortgage was still in his name? Who was going to pay his mortgage?

The new owner who had purchased the property at the foreclosure auction was highly skilled in this game. He immediately knocked on the door of the condo and explained to the tenants that he was now the new owner and to pay him the rent or else they would be evicted.

The tenants were confused. They consulted an attorney, but were instructed that this stranger who had appeared at their door was indeed the new owner and to pay him. The good news for the tenants was that the original lease was still in force so as long as they paid the rent, they could remain in the property.

Lance was in a real pickle now though. He wasn't collecting rent so he didn't have the money to pay the mortgage. He wasn't the owner of the property so he couldn't sell the property to pay off his mortgage.

Lance reached out to the new owner in hopes of convincing him to paying the mortgage. The new owner asked for all the information about the first mortgage and Lance thought this was a good sign that he would make the payments. Instead, the new owner simply gathered all the information to assess how much equity was in the deal and to have a way to obtain a payoff from the first mortgage in the event he ever decided to sell it.

What the new buyer did next devastated Lance. He didn't make payments to the first mortgage. Instead, he let it go past due. This buyer was calculated in his plan though because once the lease was over with the tenants, he didn't renew the lease and the tenants moved out. Then, he put the property up for sale and locked in a buyer. Although 8 months past due, the first mortgage had not officially foreclosed yet and the new owner ordered a payoff and was able to sell the property and payoff the first mortgage. In the end, he reaped a huge payday with very little upfront cash to do it.

Meanwhile, Lance was hit hard. He lost his original down payment and all the other money he had put in the property.

His credit was destroyed because of the 8 months of payments past due. He never collected a dime of profits from the deal.

Powerful and Profitable Learning Lessons

(1) Homeowner and Condo Associations are extremely powerful. Know their rules before you buy a property in an association and make sure you play by those rules. Associations have a history of not displaying any sympathy for delinquent members and going after members through any legal means possible to collect on what they are due.

(2) Keep some cash in reserves in case of calamity. Had Lance had just $10,000 extra, he would have been able to pay the special assessment levied by the condo association and avoided this disaster altogether.

Phil Pustejovsky

18. Your First Offeror is Usually Your Best One

Susie was cautious about investing in real estate. She understood that there were many potential pitfalls and didn't want to fall into any of them. She also didn't want to sit on the sidelines while everyone else benefited from the profits being made.

One of her major concerns was buying a fixer upper that needed extension work beyond her comfort level and also the secret problems that could lay hidden behind the walls. Susie, therefore, set her sights on new construction, because those homes were brand new and wouldn't have the same dangers as a physically distressed and dilapidated house.

She drove around and found some areas in her region that were full of new home construction. She would visit the model homes and talk with the agents on duty. Leaving her card, Susie explained that she was looking to invest and if any houses came up that needed to be sold fast and for a discount, to give her a call.

Susie eventually got a call from an agent who explained that they built each home custom, from the ground up, and that they had just finished one for a client who had put down $80,000 but was now unable to qualify for a loan so it was now up for sale. This builder was not in the business of holding onto inventory for long and wanted to just dump it right away at the amount that the previous clients were going to pay less $80,000.

Susie couldn't believe her ears. Here was a brand new, custom built home, at a purchase price of $80,000 less than what the previous buyers were going to pay. It was the same difference to the builder, but to Susie, it was an instant $80,000 in equity.

Susie quickly secured the financing and after putting down 20%, was the proud owner of a brand new $380,000 home for only $300,000 plus some closing costs. Her immediate reaction was to list the property for sale since this builder had not done that. "Who knows," Susie reasoned, "maybe it would sell for $400,000?"

She listed it with a real estate agent at $399,900 and the very next day, received an all cash offer of $350,000. "That was easy!" exclaimed Susie. But before she agreed, she wondered if it was a low ball all cash buyer that was trying to play her for a fool. So, Susie countered at $375,000. The buyer countered back with the same $350,000. Susie thought long and hard and declined the offer. Her reasoning was that if she got a $350,000 offer in one day, if she waited patiently, she may easily get $375,000 or maybe even more.

Her listing agent was disappointed because it was going to be a quick $10,500 for her too. Cash buyers are far more likely to close because there are no loan underwriters to appease. The agent was optimistic too that higher offers may come so the property remained on the market.

Although there was a flurry showings the first two weeks, the activity level dropped significantly thereafter. A month into the listing, the two deliberated and thought it best to drop the price to $379,900. No offers came in. A month later, the price dropped again, this time to $369,900. Still no offers. After making a few empty house payments, Susie was beginning to think that maybe her initial $350,000 cash offer wasn't so bad after all.

Meanwhile, the builder had another prospective buyer default and offered the deal to Susie but she was already over extended on the first deal so she passed on it. He listed it for much less than Susie's property and sold it right away. The builder had taken a buyer that may have made an offer on Susie's house by having a much lower list price.

That experience introduced Susie to the power of a low list price. She then ended her listing with her first agent and hired a new agent. With the new listing, she lowered her asking price to a humbling $339,900 in hopes of repeating what she saw the builder do. But, no offers came.

As the months wore on, a larger storm was brewing on the horizon. There was talk that the real estate bubble was bursting. Builders had over built, buyers had used interest only and negative amortization loans to purchase homes they couldn't otherwise afford with standard 30 year amortization loans, and a domino effect was occurring from all these factors that was sending real estate values into a tailspin. People were beginning to panic.

Susie didn't want to get caught so she dropped the price to $299,900. Eureka! She got an offer of $280,000 and without hesitation, she accepted. After commissions and closing costs, she lost most of her original 20% down payment but sold before the real estate market completely collapsed. Had she accepted the offer from the original offeror, she would have not only gotten her entire down payment back, but also would have reaped a profit of $23,000 in less than two months.

Powerful and Profitable Learning Lessons

(1) You first offeror is usually your best one. Typically, if you get an offer on a property you are selling right away, it doesn't necessarily indicate that there are many other buyers out there too. Instead, it is usually the result of a buyer having waited for a deal just like yours in your area for some time and therefore, when it hits the market, they move quickly. Although the actual initial offer contract may need to be countered in regards to price or terms, the offeror itself is usually your best one.

(2) Pigs get fed and hogs get slaughtered. Don't get greedy.

(3) You can't go broke taking a profit. Even if the total profit is not as much as you hoped, making even a small profit is typically the best business move.

19. Friends and Flipping

Ricky and JP had been friends since elementary school. They grew up together, went to the same college together, but Ricky got an engineering degree while JP got his undergraduate and then went onto law school. Now in their twenties, they partied together, and dreamed of the day when they wouldn't have to work and could just do whatever they wanted whenever they wanted. Over beers, they would talk about flipping houses, but with no money and very little experience, they didn't take any action on the idea.

They were both saddled with plenty of student loans, and although attorney JP was making more than engineer Ricky, neither were able to save up much money. But that all changed, when through a death in the family, JP inherited a few hundred thousand dollars.

At first, JP didn't do anything with his new found wealth. But slowly, the talks of flipping houses came up over long tailgating afternoons and eventually, Ricky made the first move and submitted an offer on a foreclosure. When it got accepted, Ricky presented a simple plan to JP; Ricky would do all the work, JP would bring the money, and they would split the profits 50/50.

The cost to purchase plus the fix up expenses would use up the vast majority of the cash JP had inherited. JP knew that Ricky had never done a house flip before but he knew Ricky was real handy and could fix just about anything. Plus, as an engineer, he was smart at organizing a project and taking care of the details. After careful consideration, JP pulled the trigger and funded the deal.

In their minds, the profit potential of the deal was enormous. At a purchase price of $175,000 and an expected $30,000 in renovations, this house could easily sell for $250,000, if not significantly more, depending on what was done to the house. After closing, JP went back to his normal lifestyle, and Ricky went to work on the house.

To save money, Ricky planned on doing most of the renovation himself. Plus, he wanted to gain the experience and thought it would be fun. At first, the project was a blast for Ricky. Working with his hands and seeing his vision come to life was far more satisfying than his current engineering desk job that required him to design complicated commercial HVAC systems for hospitals behind computer screens.

The work had to be done on nights and weekends though. Ricky was single so he had full discretion over his time when he wasn't at his day job. It was the off season for football anyway so he wouldn't be missing any game day tailgating either.

Like any significant rehab project, Ricky ran into all kinds of problems that he didn't expect. He would keep JP up to date with what was going on and the challenges he faced, but JP stayed out of it. As far as JP was concerned, he was the money piece of that puzzle and that's all he needed to do.

Night after night, weekend after weekend, Ricky worked really hard on the house. Slowly, he began to grumble to himself about JP never doing anything. The initial business plan of JP bringing the money and Ricky doing the work sounded good, but now that he was in the thick of things, the arrangement seemed very one sided. Ricky was basically sacrificing his entire life, slaving away on this project, while JP was out partying and having a good time. At the end of the day, they both stood to make the same amount of money.

As almost all first time renovations do, the cost overruns put the project on a track to blow the original budget out of the water. In part, the extra expenses were the result of problems that they didn't know existed when they first bought the house, such as rotted wood behind some walls, and other such hidden dangers that even a home inspector would never have be able to detect. But, the other issue with exceeding the budget occurred because Ricky made some decisions that would cost more than originally planned but, in his mind, would greatly improve the resale value of the house. The more changes he made, the more changes he needed to continue to make because as his improvements increased in quality, applying lower grade finishes would look stupid and stick out like a sore thumb.

Ricky shared with JP that more money would be needed to finish the project than was originally planned. What Ricky didn't realize was that JP had basically spent the rest of what little he had left. JP was tapped out.

Tensions began to rise. JP blamed Ricky for exceeding the budget on extra things that were not agreed upon in the original renovation plan. Ricky blamed JP for being completely absent from the project and leaving Ricky to make the decisions by himself which ultimately increased the budget. Meanwhile, the house was 90% finished, and in order to at least get back what had been invested, it needed that final 10% completed.

JP had terrible credit. Back in college, he had taken out some credit cards, charged them to the max at bars, made the minimum payments just long enough to get his law school student loans, and then stopped paying on all his debt. He thought he could outsmart his creditors by filing bankruptcy but those creditors had been around a lot longer than JP. It turns out, laws were enacted within the bankruptcy code to prevent students from bankrupting on student loans. Although JP was able to whip out his credit cards, all of his student loans were due and now they were in serious default with tons of late fees. JP was in no position to be able to borrow any money.

Ricky, on the other hand, had great credit and at this point, it was their only solution. Ricky got a personal line of credit from his bank based on his credit and job. Thankfully, that was all the extra money needed to get the deal to the finish line.

The property was professionally staged and it was truly a work of art on the day it was listed. Ricky and JP were pleasantly surprised to get a full price offer within a week of listing it. The closing was coming up and now that they could see a closing statement, it was time to divvy up the profits.

This is when the real drama unfolded. It was a handshake arrangement and JP's responsibility was to bring the money. He failed to bring all the money and Ricky had to step in and come to the rescue. Ricky had done all the work for free and had they hired a general contractor, the normal fee a contractor would have charged along with the costs for his subs would have taken up all the money that was now a profit.

Ricky argued that he deserved the $20,000 profit that remained after all expenses, commissions and closing costs. JP was fine with collecting $10,000 but giving Ricky all of it was not an option. JP argued that he could have made a whole lot more investing his money elsewhere during the nearly year it took to complete the project. Ricky retorted that had it not been for him, he would have blown all that money at bars and partying. It got real person as they locked horns all the way up until the day of closing. In order not to lose the buyer amidst their feud, they landed on splitting the profits 50/50.

In the end, Ricky and JP stopped hanging out. That one deal ruined a lifetime of friendship. Being that they had friends within the same circle, they would run into each other from time to time, but it was never the same again.

Powerful and Profitable Learning Lessons

(1) A real estate flip can destroy a lifelong friendship or family relationship. If you decide to do a deal with a friend or family member, put together a written agreement before you start that spells out who is responsible for what and what happens when things don't go as planned.

(2) You can get a steal of deal on a car, or even a piece of real estate, but if a partnership is too one sided and one partner has gotten a much better arrangement than the other, it'll rarely work out.

(3) It is very easy for larger renovations to go way over budget. The more work that needs to be done, the more surprises you can run into and the more tempting it can be to over-renovate. You must be disciplined and stick to your original plan because that's usually when you are the least emotional about the decisions. Once you are months into a project, you sometimes make emotional decisions over rational ones.

20. The Allure of Something Different

Tom was a very successful shopping center developer. A regular at the International Council of Shopping Centers (ICSC) conference held in Las Vegas every year, Tom knew all the players in the business, had strong relationships with the best big box retail tenants and consistently hit homeruns on the deals he developed. For the most part, he didn't venture more than about 100 miles from where he lived for his projects either.

His hometown was quite small when his career first began some 30 years ago, but steadily grew and many of the retail centers around were built by Tom. His formula was simple, yet profitable. He would start by getting confirmation from an anchor tenant exactly where they were looking to add a new location. Next, he would find a suitable property and develop the shopping center. Once the anchor tenant had moved in, he would lease out the remaining units in the center until the property was fully occupied. Then, he would sell the property and finally, he would get the management contract from the new buyers on the property. It had taken him a career to master this formula but he was now at a point whereby he had the massive down payments required to get bank financing on new projects and a gigantic cash flow pouring in from those management contracts to afford a lifestyle that included being able to fly in a private jet to the several vacation properties he owned.

The main attraction in his area over the past several years had been a stadium that was used several times a year for large events. It would bring enormous crowds for brief periods of time and the boost to the local economy was huge. Across the street from that stadium was a junk yard that had been owned and operated by the same old man for as long as Tom had been in real estate.

Anytime a deal popped up in his area, Tom knew about it quickly and the competitive person that he was, didn't want another developer to get it. Eventually the old man passed away and his heirs put the property up for sale. The asking price was very high and the property sat without an offer for quite some time. Tom got a call one day from a local government official inquiring as to if Tom had any interest in developing the junk yard property across from the stadium. "Of course," said Tom, "but the owners have priced it too high."

The governmental official, Don, had grown up with Tom. They played T-ball together when they were 5, played football together in high school, and now their kids played together on the same sports teams. Don had an idea. He shared with Tom that the government could offer an enormous property tax incentive if he developed the property. The way it would work is that the current property tax bill on the property as a junk yard would remain the same, even after the development was finished and the property was worth ten million more in value. The reason why the government would offer such an incentive would be to encourage development of that property (instead of stadium attendees seeing an ugly junk yard across the street) and if a big box retail anchor was stationed there, it would also bring many more jobs to the community. Plus, those new businesses would provide tax revenue for the government.

Reduced property taxes played a key role in how much Tom could resell the property for once a project was complete. Shopping centers are valued based on their net income, calculated by totaling all the rental income and subtracting all the expenses. Property taxes are a very large expense. If that expense is reduced, it increases the value of the center and therefore how much Tom can sell it for.

After Don had shared the finer details of the discount amount, including the 10 year reduction period, Tom went to work on running the numbers. Although he would have to offer slightly less than the junk yard heirs' asking price, he thought a deal could happen. And, to his delight, his offer was accepted.

Once Tom had a contract in place, he went to work on the full scale due diligence studies required to prepare for such a mammoth undertaking. The results confirmed his estimates that this deal would work, even without the periodic tidal wave of people that the stadium created. He lined up financing through the same regional bank that he had worked with for many years and although he would have to pay cash for the land, once the development started, the bank loan money would start to kick in.

After closing, his first steps would be to go through the planning and building departments of the local governments to get the appropriate permits and other permissions to embark on the work. Rather than quick and easy, like so many of his previous projects had been in that area, he ran into a serious problem. The government changed their mind. They wouldn't be extending Tom the property tax incentive after all. The new budget had just been approved and the government needed more money to balance that new budget.

Tom was furious. Storming into the office of his old friend, Tom demanded that the original agreement stand. "Sorry Tom, but this is outside of my control," was all he got as an explanation. As he left the office, Tom re-learned the same lesson yet again, "always get it in writing." The lesson was even more painful because this wasn't the first time in his real estate career that he had relied on a handshake rather than getting the agreement on paper with signatures.

Tom's first reaction was to just sell the property, but he would probably lose a significant amount of money if he did so he began to think through some alternatives. The zoning was quite flexible so he wasn't stuck with only being able to build a shopping center. The most feasible approach would be a property that could be sold so that the increase in value from the improvements wouldn't require him to pay for the increased property taxes. Instead, if he sold the property, the higher property tax bill would be the new buyer's problem. He also loved the residual revenue he collected from the management fees and depending on the property type, he may not get the chance for a management contract. After ruminating on it for a while, he came with an idea that would marry all these ideas together. Condos were the answer

With a condo development, he could potentially pocket a huge profit since the cost per unit to build could be far less than each unit's final sales price. The new condo owners would be paying the property taxes and plus, he could get the management contract from the condo association. He patted himself on the back for turning what could have been a giant loss into a potential homerun. Based on the price he paid for the land and the cost to build, the condos would need to be on the more luxurious side, but it sure seemed do-able. The only question now was this: Would people want to buy condos at that location?

Tom would have to pump some money into his idea to even see if it would work but he had a hunch it was worth the extra cost to explore it. He hired an architect to draw up some plans.

Using those renderings, he had a huge sign constructed announcing these luxury condos to be built and printed some marketing materials. Next, he set up a sales office in a portable trailer on the property and hired a sales agent to sell the pre-construction condos from the office. If at least 50% of the condos were sold before breaking ground, the bank would finance the project and for Tom, if he could get the loan, he would move forward with the deal.

The stadium held one of its biggest events of the year and Tom was ready to see if his idea would work. And to his shock, it actually did. Pre-construction condo buyers would sign purchase agreements and put down significant deposits. Tom thought his sales agent was super woman and gave her a raise. It didn't take long for the entire building to get sold.

The response was so overwhelming, that Tom had to adjust his plans and find a way to get two condo buildings on the property. There was plenty of acreage so fitting in a second building was easily added to the plans. The bank approved the loan and construction on the first building began.

The demand remained strong and he began taking contracts on the second building until it was 50% sold. For construction efficiency and cost reduction, Tom went ahead and started developing the second building before the first was finished.

Although most of the buyers' names were natural persons, there were a few LLCs and other legal entity buyers mixed in as well but he didn't think much of it. After all, he owned several vacation properties himself and they weren't owned in his person name.

Building One finished first. Some units took longer to finish than others because some buyers chose fancier upgrades than others. As soon as the first few buyers closed, Tom could finally breathe a sigh of relief. Rather than the government getting the best of him, Tom had outsmarted them all and done so on a property type that he had never developed before. He felt it was his finest hour and he was invincible. Or so he thought...

A peculiar thing began to happen on the project. He noticed that the majority of the new owners were putting their units up for sale soon after closing. "That's strange," Tom thought, "why are so many trying to sell units they just bought?"

Then, those for sale units began to effect the project. Subsequent buyers started running into financing issues. Conventional mortgage underwriting guidelines typically have rules related to how many condos within a development can be owner occupied as well as how many can be up for sale. There were very few units with owner occupants and almost every non-owner occupied unit was up for sale.

It dawned on Tom that the people who had signed those pre-construction contracts were primarily speculators; people who were gambling that once the condos were complete, they would sell for much more than the pre-construction price. He also figured out that his sales agent had used this angle to sell the majority of the prospective buyers. That same "super woman," was now their listing agent for the completed units.

The second building finished just in time for the buyers to begin pulling out and not closing. Most of them had also bought with the plan of reselling as soon as the units were finished but when they saw that the Building One units were not selling, they ran. Building Two was basically vacant.

It became a complete nightmare for Tom. Building One for sale units were sitting on the market for months with no showings. It wasn't just a high list price that was causing the lack of interest either. The real problem was the complete lack of demand. There just wasn't many people who wanted a luxury condo across from that stadium.

The condo owners felt they had been scammed by the sales agent and they refused to pay monthly condo association dues. With a condo association in such poor financial health along with the lack of owner occupants and so many units for sale, no banks would lend on the condos.

Some of the condos went to foreclosure and sat empty as bank owned properties. The prices of the foreclosures dropped so low that a few cash buyers came and purchased a few of the units in Building One. Over 75% of all the units were still owned by Tom and the monthly payments on his $10M loan were beginning to really affect his finances. Not to mention he had $4M of his own cash into the deal.

The big challenge for Tom was that he had personally guaranteed this loan. Unlike his shopping center loans, which were nonrecourse (and therefore if he defaulted, would not affect his personal finances), with the condo development loan, if he defaulted, the bank could take everything he owned.

He sold his jet, sold his vacation properties, and shut down or sold any other business ventures that weren't highly profitable to shore up some cash. His bread and butter business of shopping center development had to continue or else he could face complete financial breakdown, but the word got out that his condo deal was a complete flop and his bank financing was drying up.

The cash sales of some of the condos had begun to establish a market value and Tom's holdings equaled about $4M total. He contacted the bank and requested a reduction in the principal balance from $10M to the current property value of $4M. Tom explained that everyone was losing on this deal. He would be out at least $4M of his own cash too. Once the loan was modified, he would then drop the prices of the condos he owned and sell them off until the loan was paid off.

Tom thought the bank was going to approve the loan modification but in a shocking twist, the note had been sold to a note buyer for $3M! Tom couldn't believe it. Instead of getting at least $4M, without any correspondence with him on the matter, they sold their note for $1M less. As the note holder, the bank had the right to sell it for however much they wanted, but he certainly didn't see that coming.

After processing what he had just learned, Tom got excited. He reasoned that if the new note holder had paid $3M, then asking that organization for a loan modification to $4M would be a much easier request.
Tom was wrong again. The note buyer turned out to be linked to an organized crime syndicate and this was their specialty. They bought notes at a fraction of the total amount and then used all means necessary to collect the full amount from the borrowers. They had no compassion, no remorse and no guilt. They were aggressive debt collectors who knew the laws very well and had a reputation for collecting far more than anyone else in their industry.

What had taken Tom 30 years to accumulate could be wiped away on this one deal. He contacted a very well respected attorney to take on the case and defend him against the new noteholder. The case lingered on for years. Tom's legal expenses totaled $1.5M before the noteholder finally settled at $5M. Once it was all over, Tom had lost nearly $7M.

Thankfully, he was able to continue developing shopping centers during all that time and is doing quite well again, back in the business where he belongs.

Powerful and Profitable Learning Lessons

(1) Get everything in writing. Unlike some industries whereby verbal contracts hold up in court, with real estate, if it's not in writing, it's not part of the agreement.

(2) Be very cautious and careful when stepping into a completely new facet of real estate. Obviously to grow, you must step outside of your comfort zone, but you also need to be wise in how you enter an entirely new side of real estate. Tom's expertise was in big box retail shopping centers. That's where he started his career and that's where he had made all his money. As he discovered, condo development was an entirely different business altogether with its own nuisances. At the very least, he should have enlisted a highly experienced mentor in that vertical to teach him all the things he didn't know he didn't know.

(3) If you think you're invincible, you may be on the verge of a catastrophe. Tom's confidence turned into arrogance and it blinded him to the storms brewing on the horizon.

(4) Avoid personally guaranteeing business loans. That advice has been given to entrepreneurs and investors for centuries. It's a simple concept but it is often ignored.

(5) The bigger the deal, the more you can lose.

21. Scaring Away the Competition

Lester was brand new to real estate investing. He had read a few books, watched some videos online, and had talked to several different real estate professionals about flipping houses. The more he thought he learned, the more confused he became. The information seemed to be conflicting, depending on who he talked to regarding the topic

He wanted to get out of his dead end job and make a lot of money without having to kiss up to any boss. One day, he was having a particularly bad experience at work and his boss gave him some orders to do something that was completely useless in Lester's mind. Lester was convinced he was ten times more qualified to manage his department than his stupid boss. Although slightly unplanned, Lester looked his boss right in the eye and told him he could take this job and shove it!

His co-workers couldn't believe it. The typically mild mannered Lester had had enough and he wasn't going to take it anymore. The boss immediately told him he was fired and Lester responded, "Too late, I quit."

Young and unemployed, rather than go find another job, Lester decided he was going to start wholesaling houses, a technique he had learned about from all his research into real estate investing. The concept appealed to him because it seemed so simple. All he had to do was find a property seller willing to get rid of their house at pennies on the dollar, he would then have them sign a contract and as soon as he had the official contract in hand, he could then wholesale the deal to another investor.

He had read where a typical wholesale might earn $5,000. Taking out his calculator, he reasoned that if he only closed one deal every two months, he easily could pay all his measly bills. And better yet, if he did more than that, he'd be rolling in the dough.

Lester was clueless as to how to find anyone willing to basically give their house away, but one of the books he read mentioned something about knocking on the doors of people in pre-foreclosure since most investors mailed letters. He had all the time in the world so driving around and knocking on doors fit right into his schedule.

He hit the pavement and began his new career. He was petrified to talk to strangers, but with each experience, he got more and more comfortable. Lester had no idea if he was saying the right thing but he had no money to invest in his real estate investing education so he had no choice but to figure it out on his own.

Even a blind squirrel finds a nut sometimes. Lester knocked on the door of a seller who was at her wits end and simply wanted to walk away from her house. He was shocked that a seller finally said, "Yes" to signing his contract.

Lester had no idea if the deal was any good but at least he had found someone to sign a contract. Immediately, he called the number on a "We Buy Houses" sign attached to a telephone pole near the property to try to wholesale it. The person he talked to seemed really nice and agreed to come look at it.

Derek had been investing in the area for many years and supposedly had deep pockets and could close quickly if the deal was good. After seeing the property, Derek told Lester that an offer would be coming shortly. Lester was elated. And needed the money very badly. Lester eagerly waited for the offer.

The offer didn't come. Lester tried to contact Derek a few times but they all went to voicemail. Lester was just about to try contacting some other investors when he got a call from the state real estate commission. They were investigating a complaint that he was practicing real estate without a license and asked if he would be willing to come down to their office for a meeting.

The last thing Lester wanted to do was get in legal trouble. He immediately agreed to be as cooperative as possible and set up the meeting. After the call, Lester called some of the professionals that he had first met and they all told him that he should get a lawyer. Lester was broke. He couldn't afford a lawyer.

The state real estate commission reviewed his contract with the seller, his testimony as well as the notes they had in the file. It was determined that Lester was, indeed, practicing real estate without a license. The investigator cited some case law examples from the past 20 years, all of which was way above Lester's head, and explained that the penalties could be extremely severe.

Lester got down on his knees, with tears in his eyes and begged the investigator to let him go. He made Lester beg a while before telling him that since it was his first offense, Lester could go, but the contract with the seller would have to be cancelled immediately.

Lester had never been so relieved in his life. He contacted the seller, cancelled the contract, and counted his blessings for not being fined or experiencing an even larger legal penalty.

The whole experience had turned him off from real estate investing and he began to think that his dead end job was much better than being in legal hot water!

He landed a new job, making less than before, but at least he had some money coming in. With time now to reflect on the wholesaling stint he had embarked on, he got online and began researching the topic. He stumbled upon the author's website, FreedomMentor.com, and an article on the legality of wholesaling. What he discovered was very different from what the investigator had told him. He was used to conflicting information in the world of real estate investing but the way the article was written, he could tell that what was being communicated may be the truth.

Lester pulled out the official paperwork from the real estate commission that cited the case law. He posted a question in the comment section at the bottom of the webpage including some of what was written in the letter, in hopes of getting a response. The response came back that the commission had cited case law in regards to option agreements, and not bi-lateral purchase agreements. The commission had not interpreted the law correctly.

Lester didn't quite believe it at first. Since he had a job and was bringing in some money now, he decided to put his curiosity to rest and located an attorney who specialized in real estate investing to make sense of the matter. The attorney said the same thing as the comment response. What he had been doing was legal all along. The commission was using incorrect case law to support their position.

While Lester was trying to gather his thoughts on this new information, something else occurred to him. Who filed the complaint? During all the drama, it never occurred to him to even ask the question. He had just assumed it was the seller.

First, Lester called the commission to find out who filed the complaint but they wouldn't disclose that information. Next, he called the seller and thankfully she still had the same number. He could hear in her voice that she authentically had no idea what he was talking about. In fact, she was devastated that he cancelled the contract but only a few days later, a guy named Derek stopped by and he thankfully ended up buying it.

"Derek!" thought Lester. He was the only other person on the planet who even knew about that deal. It had to be him who filed the complaint. Lester later learned that the deal was right in the center of Derek's farm area and Derek was a wholesaler himself. The seller was mistaken and she didn't realize that Derek wholesaled the property to someone else.

Derek had been around the block and discovered that the easiest way to get rid of his competition was to scare them so severely that they would happily leave without a fight. Lester had fallen right into his master plan, just like other newbie wholesalers before him. Unfortunately, Lester couldn't pay him back by doing the same thing to him because Derek was a licensed real estate agent. Instead, he saved up his money and eventually invested into a real estate investing mentoring program that showed him how to beat the Dereks of the world to the best deals and to do business honestly, ethically, and morally. *(Yet another shameless plug for the Freedom Mentor Apprentice Program.)*

Powerful and Profitable Learning Lessons

(1) If you don't understand the legality of the real estate investing you are undertaking, you are at a huge disadvantage. Either hire the right attorneys or work with the right people who already understand the law.

(2) Any niche within real estate investing that is profitable typically already has entrenched competition. In order for you to be successful, you have to compete and/or beat them. To do that, you must really know what you are doing. Hard work alone doesn't cut it.

(3) The real world of real estate can be cut throat. It doesn't mean you have to be cut throat yourself, but you do need to know how to defend yourself.

(4) Real estate is not for the faint of heart. It can be incredibly profitable and enriching, but most successful real estate professionals do develop thick skin.

Learning from Deals Gone Bad

You have just learned extremely valuable lessons on real estate investing without the costs that the participants who experienced them had to go through. You literally acquired millions of dollars in education for the price of this book. Make sure you don't forget them!

It is encouraged to revisit the Powerful and Profitable Learning Lessons at the end of each story throughout your real estate investing career. As the 30 year veteran developer Tom ran into when he failed to get everything in writing, you don't want to learn the same lesson twice. It can be easy to forget them when you are in the throes of the business so read them over and over until there is no way they can slip your mind when you most need them.

There are tremendous profits and extraordinary financial success to be had in real estate investing, but you can't expect to reap those rewards without education. An overarching theme you may have discovered while reading the 21 stories is the power of having a mentor and working with someone or a team of people who really know what they are doing. It has been proven that nothing accelerates your learning of any skill better than a mentor. Sure, reading books, watching informative videos, and taking courses can help you gain some of the necessary knowledge. But, it's not until you work with a mentor that you will have your breakthrough.

I'm so passionate about the power of mentor because of the impact it had on my life. In the book, "How to be a Real Estate Investor," you'll discover my journey from being homeless to becoming an extremely wealthy real estate investor. Nothing is held back, including nitty gritty details like living off a case of Bushes Baked Beans for a month all the way to finding a buyer on my first deal with special help from some prancing deer. In addition to my story, you'll also learn the many ways that people succeed in real estate and how you can too. Best of all, you can get a free copy of "How to Be a Real Estate Investor" at www.freedommentor.com

Also, please don't forget to go to www.realestateinvestinggonebad.com to ask questions about any of the stories you read about or to share your stories of any deals that went terribly wrong. I wish you all the best in your real estate investing endeavors.

Your Freedom Mentor,

Phil Pustejovsky

Made in the USA
Lexington, KY
09 January 2018